The Secrets of Color in Hand-Hooked Rugs: Your Complete Guide to Selecting and Choosing Color

by Betty Krull with Susan Huxley

Coventry, 36" x 24", #6-cut wool on rug warp. Designed by Katherine Porter. Hooked by Betty Krull, Greer, South Carolina, 2003.

DEDICATION

To Nancy Elliot, who opened the gate that led to this most colorful path. Special thanks to my rug hooking students in South Carolina and in rug schools; without you there could not be this book. To Beth and Jim Croup, Joyce Krueger, and Sharon Townsend, special friends who have pushed, prodded, and applauded. And to my most colorful accomplishments, my children Pat, Cheryl, Jim, and Janette; they have filled my life with every value and intensity of every color.

Table of Contents

**The Secrets
of Color in Hand-Hooked
Rugs: Your Complete
Guide to Selecting and
Choosing Color**

by Betty Krull with Susan Huxley

Editor
Virginia Stimmel

Book Designer
CW Design Solutions, Inc.

Assistant Editor
Lisa McMullen

Chairman
M. David Detweiler

Publisher
J. Richard Noel

Content produced by
*Huxley Communication LLC, Easton,
Pennsylvania*

Developmental and Substantive Editor
Susan Huxley

Poetry Editor
Rachelle Redford

Photographer
Robert Gerheart

Editorial Assistant
Dorothy Smith

*Author portrait shot on location at The
Lafayette Inn, Easton, Pennsylvania,
www.lafayetteinn.com*

Presented by

**R·U·G
HOOKING**

1300 Market St., Suite 202
Lemoyne, PA 17043-1420
(717) 234-5091 • (800) 233-9055
www.rughookingonline.com
rughook@paonline.com

PRINTED IN CHINA

From the Editor

One of the most difficult aspects of designing a rug is the color planning. What colors look good together? How do you decide what colors will enhance the designs in the rug and what colors make the design recede? During the past two years, each time we have mailed a book survey to our readers, this topic has been chosen as the number one request. As a result of the survey, *Rug Hooking* magazine is pleased to present our newest book, *The Secrets of Color in Hand-Hooked Rugs*—a comprehensive book on color theory and color planning. Now, for the first time, there is a color book specifically for rug hookers.

Color surrounds us in our everyday lives. But, do you ever wonder how to apply nature's theory to our own lives—especially when planning that special rug? Take the guesswork out of it. With *The Secrets of Color in Hand-Hooked Rugs* as part of your library, the process will no longer be intimidating. Author Betty Krull will lead you step-by-step through the intricacies of each component of the process from understanding color to discovering composition, developing color harmonies, and color planning your rug. Betty further lends her expertise by providing valuable rug hooking tips in each chapter.

This book is an indispensable tool that you won't want to be without. Plus, included with the book is a handy pull out color wheel that can easily be taken along as a reference guide wherever you go.

May this beautifully illustrated book be your guide to enhancing your rug hooking experiences. Written in an easy-to-read format, each chapter of *The Secrets of Color in Hand-Hooked Rugs* will help to demystify the hows and whys of choosing the right colors to work together. Enjoy reading *Rug Hooking* magazine's newest addition. We send our very best wishes in color planning your next project.
—*Ginny Stimmel*

ABOUT THE AUTHOR

Betty Krull

If you pricked Betty's finger, her blood would flow with the colors of the rainbow. This is a woman who feels color and has a passion for it.

Throughout the country you'll find rug hookers who have benefited from Betty's color theory class, or who dream about learning from this expert. For in a world where many rug hookers have advanced color skills, Betty stands out from the crowd.

Her color course has become a classic since its introduction at the Dogwood Chapter of the Association of Traditional Hooking Artists (ATHA) in Atlanta, Georgia, in 1998, and then at the Southern Teacher's Workshop in 1999 at Ripley, West Virginia. Filled with practical, in-depth color information and theory, it's specifically designed for rug hookers. This course, she says, is the love of her life.

Now, as Betty considers retirement, she has turned her course into a book so that she can help more rug hookers create dynamic, personal rugs that deserve a second look.

Betty is a certified McGown teacher, and a member of ATHA and the National Guild of Pearl K. McGown Rug HooKrafters, Inc. She teaches from her home in Greer, South Carolina, as well as at rug schools and specialty workshops. Her articles have appeared in the ATHA magazine several times, as well as in *Rug Hooking* magazine. Betty came late to rug hooking, starting 22 years ago, but her color skills were honed many years earlier.

Back in 1976, she became a personal color consultant, learning the Munsell color system under the tutelage of the skilled colorist Don Cardwell. If you ask her, she'll say that's when she became interested in all aspects of color. But that isn't true.

Betty's color knowledge is intuitive and self-taught. Educators—and 14 years of experience dyeing fabric for braided rugs—only honed skills that had been present since Betty was a child.

As an adult, Betty's color business took her around the country for personal consultations and public speaking engagements at national conventions.

She continues to travel and teach, but now her world is focused on rug hooking. Her offerings include a three-day, hands-on color and dye workshop; a two-day hands-on dye workshop; and a one-day workshop titled "Wonderful Leaves." Her lecture subjects include "The History of Rug Hooking" and "The Color Course," but she teaches all styles of rug hooking and hooks with any cut of wool that can be used in a specific design element. Betty prefers wide-cut wool ranging from #5 to #7 blades. Both new and recycled wool can be found in her stash, which fills most of her garage.

As you read this book, Betty urges you to use your imagination to stretch yourself beyond the theory that she is presenting.

Theory is the Tool, Imagination is the Translator

"Learning from books and teachers is like traveling by carriage . . . but the carriage will serve only while one is on the high road. He who reaches the end of the high road will leave the carriage and walk afoot."—Johannes Itten, The Art of Color, *published by Reinhold Publishing Corp.*

Everyone loves color! We are constantly surrounded by color. It reflects our personality because we make color choices for our clothing, homes, and offices. It's the magic ingredient that makes such a difference in our lives. It touches every aspect of our lives and it cannot be ignored. It's everywhere, available to everyone, and so wonderfully versatile. It consistently evokes a response, creates a mood, and tunes our hearts and minds to an emotional pitch.

As we become involved in rug hooking and its many facets, we become even more aware of color. Try to imagine a world without color. Then can you, as a fiber artist, imagine your rug hooking art without color? "Art without color," says Andrew Loomis, "would lose much of its purpose." Loomis, whose career began in the 1930s, was a commercial illustrator and well-known art author and teacher.

Color is a vital part of rug hooking so it makes good sense to learn as much as we can about it. In so doing, you'll discover that it's easier to color plan and solve problems that you encounter. Your rugs will be even more beautiful. The color personalities of your hooked pieces will be more attractive, more dynamic, more stimulating, and more gratifying. When you work with color in your rug hooking, do you see it as an adventure?

Since adventures are not always as pleasing as we would wish, do you limit them with color to well-known paths, or do you look for a different route that may provide the pleasures of the unexpected? Diverse paths entice us to go beyond the familiar with a sense of excitement and the use of our imagination.

This book will give you your walking shoes, for color can be learned. The more we learn, the more developed our sense of color will be. In *The Secrets of Color in Hand-Hooked Rugs,* I'm going to give you the tools (color theory) that'll help you cultivate a discerning eye. This heightened sense of color will enable you to experiment with—and expand upon—the ways you use color.

Set some goals for yourself. Begin your adventure in color with a desire to understand it, then move on to learning the basics of color theory and how to apply color knowledge to your rugs. Analyze colors and identify their qualities. Determine to work freely with color and the color potential found in the dye pot . . . and don't forget to exercise your imagination.

CHAPTER ONE

Understanding Color

With the lessons in this book the color personalities of your hooked pieces can be more attractive, more dynamic, more stimulating, and more gratifying. This is a big promise. Its objectives, however, are well within your grasp. All you need to do is make the above statement your goal as you work your way through "Understanding Color." Reading this first chapter is the initial step in your path to developing an understanding of color theory.

The characteristics and classification of color, will take your color planning to a whole new level. You'll learn how we see color and communicate with others about it. You'll also gain an understanding of the basic (primary) colors and how these are combined to form secondary and tertiary colors.

A heightened sense of color will enable you to experiment with— and expand upon—the ways that you use color in your rugs. As you work through this chapter, you'll be developing a discerning eye. Artist Robert Henri describes this process as becoming visually literate. This is an important skill, he says, because visual literacy is the ability to not just identify problems, but to know how to solve them as well.

Southwest III, 38" x 20", #6-cut wool on linen. Designed by Gail Hill. Hooked by Sharon Richmond, Hendersonville, North Carolina, 2003. In the language of theory, this rug has only one color: turquoise. Sharon created a lovely effect by using darker and lighter values with more and less gray in them. In other words, she built a monochromatic color harmony on multiple values and intensities of one color. This rug is proof that a monochromatic color plan isn't boring. It's a challenge, perhaps, but not boring.

Sharon used a blue-green dye over gray houndstooth, gray recycled, and natural wools. Rug hookers seldom use as-is gray-and-white houndstooth. But, in this rug, the houndstooth wool stands out against the turquoise and gives the illusion of sparkling silver. Some hookers instinctively know that playing one color against another can create an interesting effect. This skill can be learned. It isn't magic, it's merely the application of color theory.

What is color? When I ask this question at the start of my Color Course class, responses vary. Some say color is "pretty," "necessary," "emotional," or that "it's *everywhere*." Others say color is "brightness," "multiple varieties," or that it needs a complicated scientific definition. A student once said that color "can be ugly, like rusty junkyard stuff." That's interesting, because I have a rusty yard art angel piece that came with a rather hefty price tag.

The scientific definition of color is pretty clear. Color is your body's response to light. Specifically, it's the sensation produced by white light rays striking the part of your eye that's called the retina, which is at the back of your eyeball. The body converts the light rays to electrical impulses that the brain interprets as color. We see so many colors because the length of these light rays varies.

Through the wonder of light, there is color. These same light rays create our world of form. There can't be dark or shaded areas without light rays. Artistically, we identify objects first by shape, no matter what color they are. Recognizing shape is a function of the intellect; color awareness is instinctive.

Color is also subjective. Consider, for example, *Southwest III*, above. A glorious celebration of turquoise, its success depends on multiple intensities and values of this one color, which is played against gray and a light value of blue green. In later chapters, I'll give you the language to describe the variations that you're admiring right now.

It's easy to understand how our conversations about dyeing can go awry . . . what I think is turquoise could be different than what you consider to be turquoise. In this chapter, you'll learn a language that'll make it easier to describe color. But before we get into that, let's discuss the role that color choices and judgments play in our rugs. Next, we'll explore how placing colors side-by-side—or overlapping—can affect our perception of color. As rug hookers, this is important because we can use color placement to create wonderful illusions in our work.

If color is such an integral part of our lives, why, when we hook rugs, are we indecisive, intimidated, and just plain frustrated? This is a normal reaction, and there are valid reasons for these feelings.

- We all see and describe color differently, and use different names for the same colors.
- Color is intangible, never absolute but relative to a total situation.
- The potential of color is multiplied when combined with another color or colors.
- Our emotions play a significant role in our response to color.

No wonder we have a tough time!

Variations Abound A single color can have an unlimited number of variations. Viewed separately, they could all be described with the same name. If the differences are subtle, and sometimes even when they're more obvious, it's only when you place several together that you discover the colors need to be further defined. Look, for example, at the photo at right.

With all of these choices, how on earth could you pick the right red for a rug? After reading *The Secrets of Color in Hand-Hooked Rugs,* color theory will be your tool for this decision. Your imagination will do the rest.

One day I was talking with a student about wool that she wanted me to dye for a rug. When I asked her to send me a color sample, she said it wouldn't be necessary because she simply wanted cranberry. Do you have any idea how many reds you can pick out of a bag of cranberries?

Wrong isn't Wrong Color is affected by our color vision and our color choices. There are no right or wrong colors, only right and wrong color choices. This *Pumpkin Boy* at right, which is part of a rug that's shown on page 64, is a perfect example. Using an analogous color harmony, everything went well until it came time to hook the boy. I gave him a wonderful sweater made with a very small piece of plaid, and then I dressed him in brown overalls. According to theory, these were the correct color choices. Yet I disliked the look. My imagination helped me decide to step out of the box. I changed the overalls to blue then hooked the bluebird. The bird is a pumpkin-breasted bluebird, the only one of its kind!

Feelings Influence Perception The color choices we make—and the way we see color—are affected by our emotions. For example, Marion O'Beirne of Simpsonville, S.C., based the color plan for her *Bethlehem* piece on page 44 on her passion for a yellow-orange and orange-red sky.

We don't consciously think about how our color likes

"What is color? All pervasive, it is carelessly taken for granted, and curiously, largely unstudied by the majority. It affects us emotionally, makes us warm or cold, provocative or sympathetic, excited or tranquil. Color enriches the world and our perception of it. A colorless world is almost unimaginable."—Donald Pavey, Color, *published by Knapp Press*

Bethlehem, 10" in diameter, #3-cut wool on burlap backing. Designed by Jane McGown Flynn. Hooked by Marion O'Beirne, Simpsonville, South Carolina, 2003.

and dislikes are shaped by the events and people in our lives. Yet we have learned responses. In rug hooking classes, I've watched some students copy a rug color plan exactly. In one instance, I later learned that someone told a student she really shouldn't pick her own colors. Her learned response was "don't try anything on your own, just copy what someone else has done. You can't do it as well." Working as a color consultant, I saw many examples of this. Mothers would tell daughters not to wear a certain color. That message carried into much of the daughters' adult life.

Think about your family. Do you find that you often decorate your home or dress in the same colors as someone else in your family? Or maybe you tend to hook rugs in colors that are similar to the ones used by others in your hooking community, or by your mentor. Use these for inspiration, but learn to develop your own sense of color and design.

Color is Intangible Despite what the fashion industry says, there's no such thing as the perfect red, or any other color for that matter. Trying to identify it would be as elusive as matching a swatch that was dyed with PRO Chem #503.

Color is never an absolute. Whatever color you look at, it will appear to be something else if the colors around it change. Look at the five photos on this page. All of the central squares are the exact same color—a mid-value red—yet they look very different when placed in context. As the name suggests, mid-value colors are in the middle of the range of light to dark. If you imagine a straight line, and place a dark red at one end and a light red, such as pink, at the other, the mid-value swatch would be positioned somewhere at the mid-point. The mid-value colors are the ones that we're most comfortable with. Be careful, though, because too many mid-value colors make boring hooked pieces.

1 In the color block, the mid-value red square is positioned over another color that's in the natural color spectrum. Orange and red are closely related colors. Thanks to an effect described as after-image, our eyes see a bit of the orange in the red and a bit of the red in the orange. In other words, the colors pick up a bit of each other. You can see this in rug hooking. I've used orange as the outline in a small, predominantly red oriental rug. This gives red more spark.

2 Placed on a strong, bright yellow, the same mid-value red appears to be orange-red. Of all five examples, this is the only place where the red takes on the appearance of a high-intensity (brighter) red. Bright yellow is difficult to work with—pale yellow and soft golds are easier to use in hooked pieces.

3 The same mid-value red loses its vitality when placed on green. These two colors are called complements, and they neutralize each other because they are both mid-value colors. When using red and green together, great care must be taken to ensure variety. This is where it's important to remember the saying, "Every rug needs a bright, a light, a dark, and a dull."

4 The blue in this combination is a pure color. The red to blends into it, so there's very little contrast between the two colors. Adding yellow would enhance both colors, because yellow adds a glow to other colors. Always keep in mind that yellow is bright and a little goes a long way.

5 Because the purple is dark, the red also appears darker. This fascinates me. Dark purples are often used for hooking shadows. A bit of dark purple in the center of a red rose, for example, gives an illusion that there's depth at the center of the flower. If you use a purple background for a rug, make certain all your colors are lighter, and look like they are laying on top of the purple rather than sinking into it.

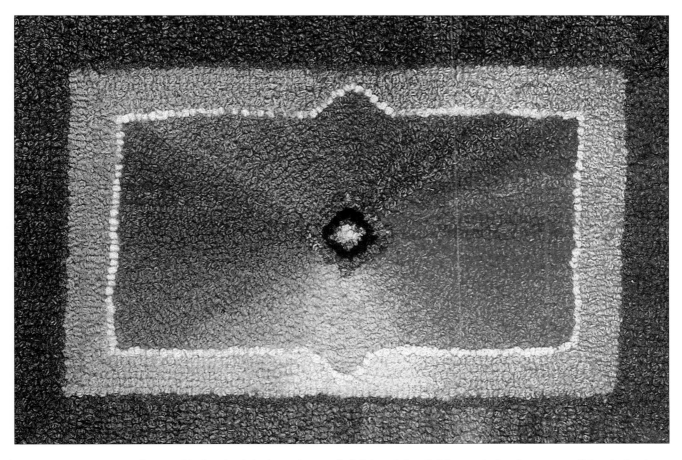

So many blues, purples, and yellows . . . this photo barely begins to show you the infinite variations that there can be in colors, or even within a single color. What great news for rug hookers, because we're always looking for the ideal skin tone, color range for fine shading a flower, or specific color for an element in a pictorial rug! Knowing that so much is available to us shows that our options are limited only by our imagination. And it's such a delight when we find that perfect piece of wool. Of course, we can expand the color palette for our rugs by dyeing wools to match.

I have a collection of old books that explore color theory. The text in one of these, which is almost 100 years old, mentions the colors leghorn yellow, ashes of roses, and elephant's breath. What in the world is ashes of roses? I'd have to burn some to figure that out. Would you like to go with me on a visit to a poultry farm to see a leghorn breed of chicken, or would you prefer a trip to the zoo to see if we can get close enough to identify the elephant's breath?

These names are long out of use, yet today, we still define color with word descriptions like Nile green and old rose. Even these common names may be different colors to each of us. Words are incomplete and change with the times. In fact, the words we use and the terms we apply to color often cause misunderstandings.

You can see that words are stumbling blocks. For us to learn more about color theory in later chapters of *The Secrets of Color in Hand-Hooked Rugs,* and talk with each other

about desired colors in our rugs, we need a common language that's less open to interpretation.

In your search for as-is wool—or as you start dyeing fabric—an understanding of color classifications is very helpful. You can learn to describe, for example, all the blues in the photo on page 10 in a way that others will understand. Plus, the color descriptions that you use will make it easier to figure out how to re-create that color in your dye pot.

In this chapter, you'll learn about the color wheel and the color star. Both of these tools will help you describe color and lead to a better understanding of how to use some basic colors to create new varieties of color when you dye your wool.

Rug hooking is visual. This fact alone makes the knowledge and uses of color our first concern. We need to learn the composition of color so that we can see its potential.

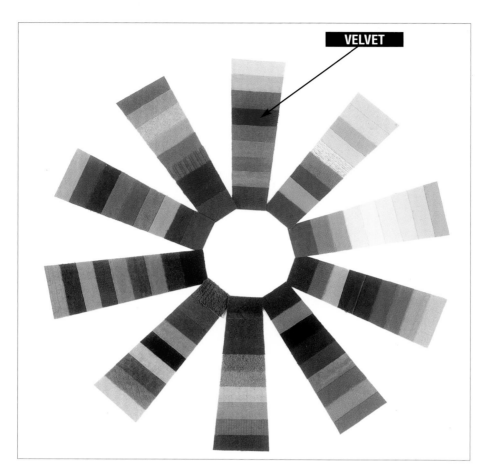

VELVET

Color Circle

Do you remember playing with a prism back when you were in grade school? Light shining through the prism would separate into a beautiful array of colors. You were probably in science class, and your teacher was explaining white light, which is sunlight. You were learning a concept that's several hundred years old.

Around 1660, Sir Isaac Newton discovered that white light consists of seven individual colors. The colors, if you remember the prism from your school days, ran in a straight band from red to purple. These are the same colors that you see in a rainbow. Sir Newton concluded that red, orange, yellow, green, blue, indigo, and violet are the natural color spectrum.

He creatively twisted that line into a circle, then combined red and violet to create an additional color which we call red-purple. This was the first color circle, or color wheel, so-called because it's an arrangement of colors around a central point. There are also colors moving out and away from the center, with each color becoming slightly darker at each step. More colors were added to the originals in Sir Newton's color wheel, so that today's version includes 12. They are yellow, yellow-orange, orange, red-orange, red, red-purple, pur-ple, blue-purple, blue, blue-green, green, and yellow-green.

Since Sir Newton offered his color wheel to the world, artists everywhere have considered it an essential tool. I would be thrilled if more rug hookers included a color wheel in their supply kit. We have many designs and backings, hooks in a variety of designs and sizes, and wools galore. We should also consider the color wheel a necessary tool for successful rug hooking.

Many artists have developed their own color wheels, each with a particular point of view about the classification of color. The only one that I recommend is the Artist's Color Wheel. This product includes a neutral gray scale and a chart that shows what will happen if you add one color to another. That feature will help when you want to overdye wool and wonder what your final color will be. It's important to be able to identify a neutral gray scale. Dyeing red over neutral gray, for example, gives you a deep red. If you use blue-gray and overdye it with red, you will have red-purple. As we increase or decrease the amount of gray in a color we obtain unlimited variations of color. Gray is a sterile neutral depending on neighboring colors for life and character. It weakens the brightness of a color and mellows it. Proceed with caution when you decide to use gray as a background color.

The color wheel on page 10 is an oldie but a goodie. I made it back in 1976, when I was a professional color consultant. This was long before I discovered the joys of rug hooking. I'll never forget this wheel, because it's made with dressmaking fabric. Note how the texture of the fabrics has an impact on the way that the colors read as you view the chart. By contrast, the color star shown at right is made with carefully dyed wool. The color is more consistent and effective.

Does anything on the color wheel jump out at you? At the 12 o'clock position, mid-way down the spoke, there's a dark red that doesn't quite fit the color range. This is a velvet, so it appears to be a darker color than it really is. The wrong side of this piece fits nicely in the range. I point this out because it's a perfect example how texture affects color.

My early color wheel is based on a Munsell version that has 10 spokes instead of 12, which is what we find on today's standard color wheel.

Color Star

Most of us learned the sequence of color on a color wheel. The wheel is important to me, and it's worth mentioning because most people will find the information on the wheel very valuable. It shows you the location of colors, which helps us with their classification.

I prefer The Color Star developed by Johannes Itten. This product, which can be found in some art and bookstores, isn't a book. It's a color wheel and eight disks with a black and a white side. The disks help me compare cool and warm values, complementary colors, and different hues and intensities. This is great for color planning because it allows me to see the color harmony I'm thinking about. It also gives me a good idea how a dark or light variation will work as a background.

Because we're interested specifically in color for rug hooking, I use the traditional color circle, which is shown at right. It's developed from the primary colors red, yellow, and blue. Combining the primaries creates all other colors. Orange, for example, is a combination of red and yellow.

Orange, green, and purple are called secondary colors. The secondary colors are marked on the star at right. They are created by mixing together two primaries. As mentioned in the primary entry, above, combining red and yellow creates orange. Red and blue make purple. Blue and yellow make green.

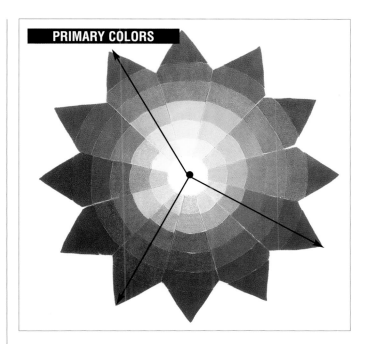

PRIMARY COLORS

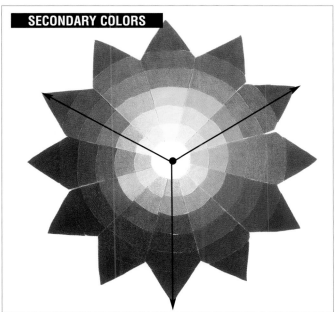

SECONDARY COLORS

▶**TIP** **The Cutting Edge**

Scissors are a critical tool for rug hookers. I have three pairs that are necessary for me. The first are a very good pair of shears used ONLY for fabric, that I use to hand-cut wool. The second are 5" bent handled scissors, kept very sharp, that I use for trimming the ends of wool as I pull them up. The smallest, but most significant are 4" very sharp pointed scissors with a short 1.5" blade. I use these for shaping when a strip of wool looks too wide. I just go in and shave off a "tad"—a good southern word. Keep your scissors well sharpened and in a protective sleeve when you store them.

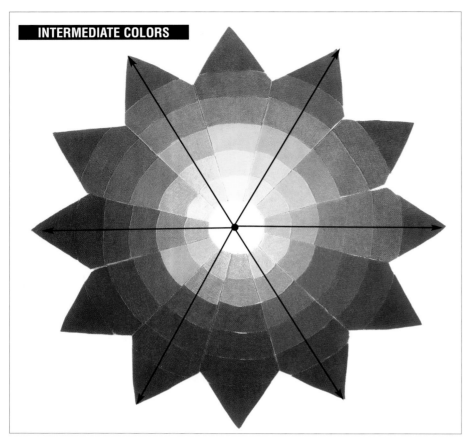

INTERMEDIATE COLORS

Tertiary, or intermediate, colors are a mix of primary and secondary colors. The tertiary colors are marked on the star at left. I tend to call these hybrids, or sophisticated, colors. In everyday life, these tertiary colors have many names. But in color theory, the tertiary colors are identified by the distinct blend of primary and secondary colors. They're known as red-orange, yellow-orange, yellow-green, blue-green, blue-violet, and red-violet.

My Favorite

I don't think it would surprise anyone to know that yet another author loves her collection of books. But I'm a rug hooker first and foremost. The books that I hold dear are the ones that talk about art, color theory, and rug hooking techniques. Some of these are old and worn, others are new.

My absolute favorite book is *The Art of Color* by Johannes Itten, published by Reinhold Publishing Corp. In the realm of color theory, the author of this book is my mentor.

My edition is from the early 1960s. As you can see by the photo at right, the pages are dog-eared and the cover is worn. When I bought it at an antique shop, it was already worn. I've read and re-read this book so many times that the pages are even more dog-eared than when I found it. If you'd like to search out Itten's work, you won't have to look hard. *The Art of Color* is still in print, as are several of his other books and his product The Color Star. (The color star is explained on page 11.)

Another book that I treasure is *Elementary Color* by Milton Bradley. This is a very old book, published in 1895. *Color in Hooked Rugs*, by Pearl K. McGown, another favorite, isn't nearly as old. *Color*, written by Donald Pavey and published by Knapp Press, is yet another one I like and is still in print.

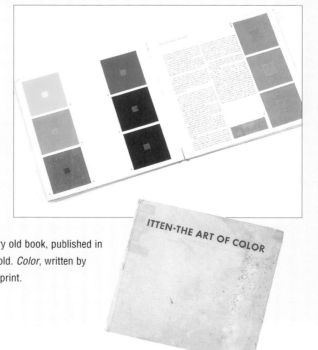

ITTEN·THE ART OF COLOR

CHAPTER TWO

Discovering Composition

In the previous chapter, you learned the cut-and-dried aspects of color. The way that our eyes register color, how hues are arranged along a natural spectrum, and the use of primaries to create all other colors are ideas given to us by chemists and scientists.

But, for rug hookers, color isn't about facts and analysis. Color is the joyous splash of red on a robin's breast, the pink blush in a rose petal, the rich purple in an evening sky . . . and how we can present these subtle effects with our hooks and wool.

It seems that we all instinctively know that developing a discerning eye will help us hook rugs that are even more beautiful than the pieces we're creating right now.

In this chapter, you'll learn the terms commonly used to explain important concepts. In so doing, you'll gain a better understanding of how color is perceived and how it can be used in your rugs. You'll also develop an understanding of the hue scale, which is a way to display the tremendous variety that can be obtained from a single color.

You need this theory as a foundation for the practical application of color that's presented in later chapters. The time spent increasing your color knowledge now will be well-spent, because rug hookers make the best color choices from basic and expanded palettes that are built on sound color theory.

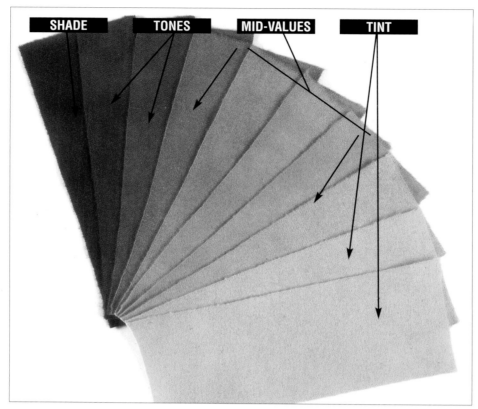

SHADE **TONES** **MID-VALUES** **TINT**

This transitional color swatch starts with a dark tone of mulberry—a red-purple, and gradually moves down through a range of nine more values that ends with an soft apricot, a yellow-orange swatch. It's considered a diagonal color path—and it's very dramatic. In traditional fine shading a swatch like this can be used for crewel designs, as well as for flower and fruit motifs. It would make very dramatic scrolls. In wide-cut hooking, use the colors as you wish, assured that all 10 values will blend well.

Try explaining the colors in the swatch shown above. On the next page, there's another swatch labeled with the terms that artists use to describe color. Don't those simple words make a world of difference?

At the turn of the century, artists, scientists—and probably rug hookers—were still struggling with ways to define color, so that they could communicate without misunderstandings. Soon, international research and meetings led to a common language. Color was given scientific numerical designations, and even more explanations were added to the work that had been done by previous generations.

As rug hookers, we don't need to get into the complex details that were laid down by these experts. But we do need to understand certain words that are used to describe color. In fact, I'll be using them throughout the rest of *The Secrets of Color in Hand-Hooked Rugs.* Soon, your conversations about color in rugs and in your dyeing will be peppered with words like hue, intensity, and value. You'll wonder how you ever did without these descriptive terms. And, every time you use the words, you'll be reinforcing your understanding of color. This happens because you'll need to assess how a specific color—or combination of colors—in a rug is composed in order to use each word.

▶ **TIP Through Thick & Thin**

It's interesting that in traditional tapestry hooking the narrow-cut of a dark color, when used for a dark background, doesn't look as heavy as the same dark color used in a wide-cut. The weight of a color is also determined by its placement. A rug with a dark center and a light perimeter, for example, creates the illusion that the edges of the rug are turning up. Adding a dark border to a rug that has predominantly light values will anchor the piece to the floor.

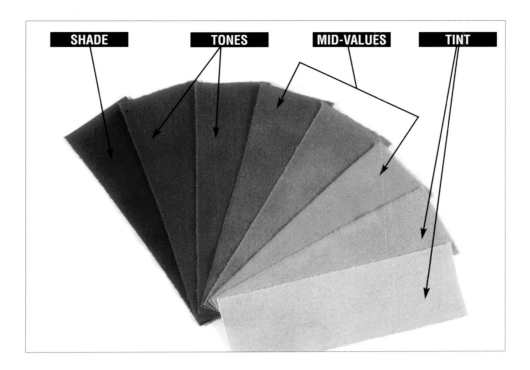

This swatch displays a range of values, spanning from dark to light. The first swatch piece is a shade, a color with more gray. Tones are beautiful rich colors with some gray, a sophisticated range of color. Mid-values form our comfort range—not too dark, not too light. Tints are colors with white or small amounts of gray.

To better understand terms used to define color generally, the definitions of these and several other color terms follow.

Hue This is, very simply, the family name for a color. Red, for example, is a hue. Your makeup containers, the cans of paint in your basement, and other color products around your home have names like Blush, Rose Stone, or Very Berry. These exotic or romantic names aren't considered hues.

Value A comparison of the amount of color in wool with a range from light to dark. In other words, value describes the lightness or darkness of a color. Yellow has a high natural value, whereas purple has the lowest natural value.

Intensity, or Chroma A description of the saturation of color is intensity. *The World Book Dictionary* describes it as "the degree of a color's freedom from white, gray or black." It is a description of the amount of pure color in a piece of wool. High intensity color is purer; yellow has a high natural intensity, purple has the lowest natural intensity.

Tint A light value of a hue is a tint. You can get a tint by adding white, or a gray that's lighter than the natural value of a color. Tints with gray have a chalk-like appearance and are commonly called pastels. Small amounts of color dyed over white yields a clean and light effect.

Mid-values A comfortable range of color from gray to pure color, never having a very high intensity.

Tone This is a color that's based on gray. Unlike a tint, in a tone the gray is darker than the natural value of the color to which its added. A tone is a rich color with a sense of stability. When used in a higher intensity with more brightness, tones can give your rug drama.

Shades As the name implies, a shade is dark. It's a dark value of a hue. Shades have more black or gray in them than pure colors. These can be used effectively for shading in a rug.

▶TIP Color It Beautiful

Shades and tones can be used to great effect in a hooked rug. When you're looking for a way to create a shadow, consult your color wheel. Pick out the color that you're considering, and then slide your finger up to a shade of that color. This will give you a suitable choice for the shadow in your rug.

High-intensity tones, on the other hand, add drama to a rug. In some instances, using a tone can also make a color more acceptable. Red-purple, for example, is a very difficult color to work with. It's best used in the deep tones.

Coventry, 36" x 24", #6-cut wool on linen. Designed by Katherine Porter. Hooked by Louise Schram, Whitehouse, Ohio, 2003. Louise wanted the flowers in her rug to stand out or, as I would say, "advance." For this to happen, the leaves had to be worked in subordinate, gray-green textures. Bright red is an excellent dominant color. Yet Louise needed to use it carefully—only in the flowers—to avoid a Christmas theme. The red in the curb line still pops, even though it's a less intense red than the flowers. Louise used pieces of a braided spot dye (see page 25) to achieve this effect. Introducing some darker, duller reds anchored the bright reds to the background. Then, to really anchor the rug to the floor, Louise added three rows of a dark green-black around the edge. Even this small amount of contrast between the dark green of the body of the rug and the green-black in the border gives an added sense of weight.

For rug hookers, color is less about matters of fact and more about emotions, feelings, and how we perceive color. When admiring a beautifully hooked rug, we speak of its overall beauty and, indirectly, the way that it makes us feel. In these conversations, we're really talking about the psychology of color: how we see some hues as more over-powering than others, how their personalities change when they're grouped in different ways, and how we attach feelings to some colors.

These more arbitrary color concepts (as compared to the scientific basis of color that we explored in chapter 1) are explained with terms like dominance, energy, weight, mood, and temperature. On the following pages, you'll learn more about these new terms. To help you understand them, detailed photos of rugs hooked by me, friends, and students are used as examples. The rug shown above, for example, deftly uses several of the concepts that are explained on the next few pages.

Red and green are a difficult combination to work with, yet Louise Schram succeeded in her version of a pattern called *Coventry*. Although she used colors we emotionally associate with Christmas, her piece isn't seasonal. She has balanced the design with the use of both colors in a variety of values and intensities. To learn more about this piece, see the caption above and read the commentary on page 68.

Dominance

The central rose in the rug at right is a good example of color and design dominance. The rose jumps to the foreground because it's the largest design element. I enhanced the effect by hooking it in colors that also command attention. The surrounding colors, which are darker, play a secondary role. This rug, called *Antique Rose*, is shown in its entirety on page 64.

When we look at rugs, some motifs appear larger than others, even if both are hooked in areas that are the same size. The motif that appears larger is considered dominant to the other. Naturally, the second color is called subordinate.

Energy and Weight

Some colors tend to pop off a rug. No matter where they're used in the pattern, they make that design element look like it's in the foreground of the finished piece. More than color dominance is at work in these instances. The effect is caused by the way we perceive colors as having energy and weight.

The energy of a color is the sense of activity or movement that we feel when we look at it. Weight is an apt description of the way that a color can give us the feeling that it's heavy, or a sense that it's lifting up off the surface.

Marilyn Denning's *Coventry*, shown at right, is a good example of the effective use of energy and weight. The depth of this rug's background sets the tone for the entire piece. The colors have great contrast yet there isn't one thing that lacks a sense of sturdiness. While the four large leaves aren't hooked in dark values, their size makes them feel substantial, like they have visual weight. The plaid used for the curb line doesn't convey a distinct color, but it gives a subtle break in the background color. This is a small pattern with large elements in the design, giving the finished rug an air of importance. You can see the entire rug, and learn more about it, on page 69.

The key thing to remember with energy and weight is that bright colors advance and dark colors recede. Dark colors feel heavy and sturdy. These are very important characteristics to remember when you're selecting colors for a rug. Weight can also be determined by the motifs in a pattern: the larger the motif, the greater the sense of weight it conveys.

"The use of color is an open-ended adventure limited only by the extent of one's imagination and sense of adventure."—Donna Sapolin, True Colors, *published by Hearst Books*

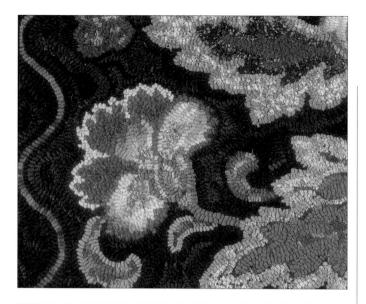

Compare the feeling of weight that's achieved by using a light or dark background, as shown in the two rugs at left. Both are the same *Coventry* pattern that Marilyn Denning hooked.

The background of my rug (top left) is a dark red-brown, which I overdyed with black. Interestingly, I was determined that this rug was going to have a light background. But when I hooked in a light value of orange that matched a leaf color, the entire rug looked flat. The color just didn't work. The dark background, on the other hand, anchored everything, gave the piece visual weight, and created an effect that made the reds glow. The entire rug is shown on page 67.

The light background in the middle rug works, whereas mine did not. This rug was hooked by Susanne McNally, and it also has brilliant colors. Against a dark brown background, the blue-green and blue-purple colors wouldn't have shown well . . . there wouldn't be any drama because there wouldn't have been enough contrast.

For the background, Susanne used natural wool with a wash of orange dye. Orange is one of the dominant colors in her rug. The curb line is a spot dye of her blue and blue-purple colors.

Why isn't the light background boring? Susanne hooked directionally, following the shapes of the motifs. For a good look at the entire rug, see page 67.

Mood

When rug hookers choose color, our selections are based primarily on personal preference. In other words, our emotions motivate our picks. Color, absolutely, has an emotional aspect. Particular hues—or variations such as a shade, tint, or tone—will tug at our hearts or heads. In other words, certain colors or combinations of colors stir up our feelings. The *Coventry* rug at (lower left), for example, brings a sense of dramatic calm to the viewer. This effect is conveyed primarily by the purple and blue-purple in the work.

This entire rug, which was hooked by Joyce Krueger, conveys a mood of motion and movement. Isn't it gorgeous? Part of the sense of motion comes from the color transitions. Joyce began with yellow-green, moved through the greens into blue-green, and then on to blue, blue-purple, and purple. Using the green, blue-green, and blue combination for the leaves encourages the viewer to think about water with ripples and waves. Our eyes then travel to the yellow-green and the tips of leaves. You can see more of this rug on page 65.

For the visually dramatic effect of one color intensifying the other, it's necessary to have differences in values and intensities. If we mix the two colors in the harmony, we almost have a neutral brown-gray color. The mood of the one color can be cancelled by its complement if they are the same value and intensity.

Temperature

Most of us can instinctively identify a color as cool or warm, even if we lack knowledge of color theory. It's something that we learned very early in life, and pass on to others for years and years. Yellow makes us think of sunlight, which is warm. Red is hot. Chocolate, coffee, and fire—all orange colors—are comforting and warm. Sky, water, and a forest display the green and blue values that we associate with cool colors.

The photo at right shows a color star that has been divided in half, straight through the middle of the yellow and purple. This division marks the split between the cool and warm colors on the color star. The left side has the cool colors while the right side shows the range of warm colors.

The line on the color wheel runs through the yellow and purple because these two colors have both cool and warm versions, as you can see in the photo (middle right).

I've noticed that there's a strong tendency among my students to move toward either a cool or warm color range. I tend to think in warm colors. For example, when I lived in New England I wore a red winter coat because I wanted the visual warmth.

I now live in South Carolina, which has a warm climate, so I use cool colors in my garden, including white flowers like azaleas, camellias, irises, and magnolias. In the heat of summer, I use white begonias and impatiens, as well as green hostas with white edged leaves. Blue and purple irises, pansies, and lots of green leaves help the garden look cool.

Of course, if some colors can be cool or warm, you're probably wondering how you should select temperatures to use in your rug. Your first color choice for a rug is usually a personal preference, or else influenced by room decor or some other inspiration. All other cool and warm color selections are based on this first color. Many rugs are a mix of cool and warm colors.

I explored the cool and warm sides of colors in one of my rugs, called *Winchester*. A portion of it is shown at right. This rug is predominantly cool with many, many leaves and scrolls in various values of green and blue-green. The white flowers are cool . . . even the ones that have a touch of purple. You can see the range of warm colors in the large flowers, which contain pink, and in the yellow used for the central rose. Veins in the scrolls are also warm, since they're predominantly red. The dark brown-black background adds warmth. For more information about this rug, see page 60.

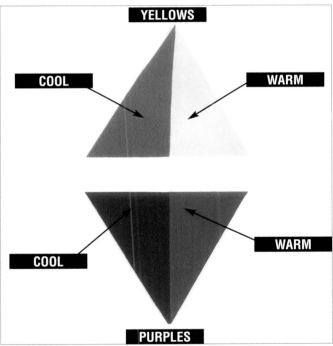

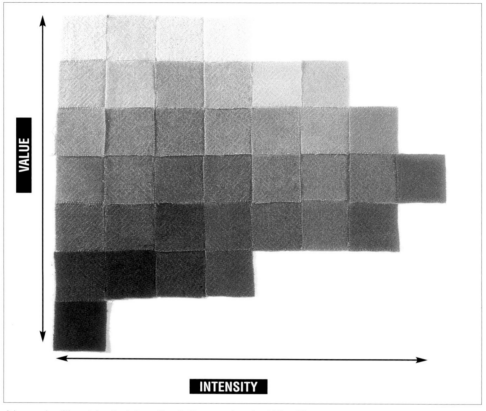

A hue scale still contains the information that's on a color wheel. The difference is the way that the variations of a color are shown. There are still mid-values, shades, tints, and tones. On a color star or wheel, the possibilities of a single hue are arranged in a straight line. Tints are closest to the center, or pole, of the star or wheel, and there's a shift toward the shades as you move outward.

The color circle and the color star are very valuable tools for any rug hooker. Yet, now that you've read through the information in "Understanding Color," you're probably starting to discover that these tools have limitations. The color circle and star don't show the variety that you can explore by playing with the intensity and values of a color. This is where the hue scale comes into play. (The photo above is an example of a hue scale for just one color.)

Unlike the color wheel, the hue scale is a relatively new invention. About 1912, artist and mathematician Albert Munsell devised a system that gives us the ability to see all color in perfect order. For every color, you can adjust the intensities and values to achieve subtle—and not-so-subtle—variations. These results are shown on the hue scale, with a vertical edge indicating values and a horizontal scale showing changes in intensity. Munsell identified each position on the scale with numbers, because he was frustrated with the lack of a standard reference for any value of any color.

While using a number identification may not seem valuable to us as rug hookers, the hue scale is still very important. In this section, I'm going to explain the hue scale and the color paths, and show you how you can use both when color planning or dyeing wool for a rug.

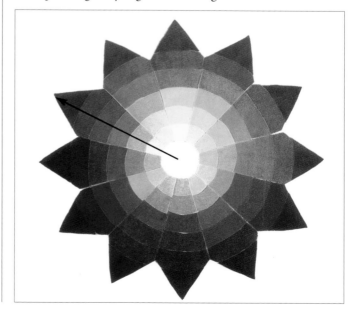

The color star, shown on the previous page, has only six values of any hue. Take a look at green, which is marked. The value closest to the center is very light, because it's a tint. Moving away from the center, there's less and less white as the values shift toward a purer version, or chroma, of green. Past this, the green samples have more and more gray in them.

The hue scale at right gives us 46 values for a single hue. That's a big difference from the handful shown on the color star. And a hue scale doesn't stop at 46. There are no limitations to what you can do by adding and reducing the gray in a color.

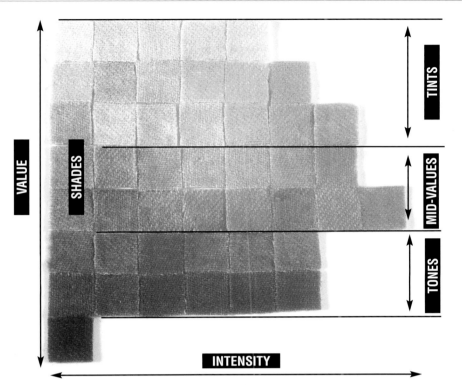

I created the hue scale at (top right) with white wool, plus a neutral silver gray and cardinal red Cushing dye that, unfortunately, are no longer available. My goal was to create a hue scale in wool, so that this tool would be more interesting for rug hookers. Now you won't have to make your own hue scale, because I've done the work for you. Nevertheless, I encourage my students to pick a color and make a hue scale because the process leads to a greater understanding of the composition of color, which, in turn, improves the color choices they make for any rug.

Color Paths

Now that you have an understanding of the possibilities of a single color, we can use this same chart to define color paths. The hue scale is made up of color paths. Trust me, this isn't all theory. Some of the rugs that are shown in *The Secrets of Color in Hand-Hooked Rugs* were developed with color plans built on color paths.

Color paths is a phrase coined by Pearl McGown in her book *Color in Hooked Rugs* There are three types: diagonal, horizontal, and vertical.

Vertical Color Path Ranging from dark to light hues, this path shows a sequence of values of one color. A vertical color path shows several values of one color. Value swatches, like the one shown at right, have been a staple of fine shading for many years. They're exceptional for hooking flowers and leaves. I also use value swatches in wide-cut rugs to provide a continuity of color within a rug. I just break up the swatch and define the values as light, medium, and dark.

> ▶ **TIP Still The One**
>
> If a certain value of color doesn't look right in a color plan, look at the hue scale and pick another value, either darker or lighter. This new choice, which is still related to your original color, could be the right one for your rug.

Horizontal Color Path The intensity (chroma) paths are along the horizontal edge of the hue scale. As shown at top left, the hues go from a deeply grayed color to a bright, pure, high-intensity color. Rug hookers are less familiar with horizontal paths. This always surprises me. In all my hooking years, I can't remember ever dying a horizontal swatch! I think that, instead, we use a backward L shape: We overdye gray with the dye from the darkest values of the vertical swatch to get the gray values found in the horizontal swatch.

Diagonal Color Path This is the most interesting color path. It stair-steps down from a tint of gray to clear chroma. I dyed this for a light pink rose. The lightest value is a very light gray which goes to mauve and gradually moves to a mid-value color range. These colors have less gray, and value 7 is pure color.

Transitional Diagonal Path A diagonal path can change from one color to another. This swatch begins with wool dyed blue and with each succeeding piece of wool an orange dye solution is added. When we use equal amounts of orange and blue, the color becomes a grayed green. As we continue to increase the orange dye, the final colors are tones of orange. Marilyn Denning used this single 12 value swatch plus an 8 value red swatch for her *Coventry* rug which you can see on page 69 .

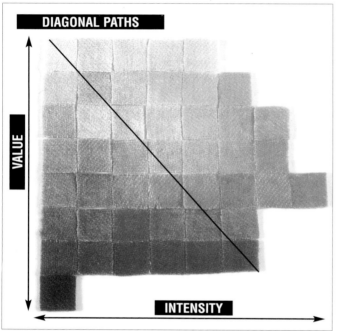

DIAGONAL PATHS

VALUE

INTENSITY

> **TIP Buy the Book**

The Secrets of Color in Hand-Hooked Rugs isn't a book about dyeing wool, so I'm not offering you formulas for creating specific colors.

Many books include basic instructions for dyeing wool. I would, however, like to tell you about my favorite resources. In these are the recipes I turn to, time and again, when I'm looking for color formulas.

My bookshelves include the following titles:

▲ *Jewel Tones* by Carolyn Clemens provides recipes for PRO Chem wash-fast acid dyes.

▲ *Primary Fusion* by Ingrid Hieronimus is sold with swatches and a PRO Chem color card.

▲ *Prisms: 64 Spots & 35 Oriental Backgrounds* and *Prisms #2: 57 Straight Gradations and 102 Transitionals*, both by Nancy MacLennan and Claire deRoos, offer dye formulas using PRO Chem wash-fast acid dyes.

▲ *Recipes from the Dye Kitchen* by Maryanne Lincoln builds on the author's popular column by the same name for *Rug Hooking* magazine. This book is full of information and new ideas.

▲ *Scraps or Spots: 115 Formulas For Rug Hooking* by Dotti Ebi is a nice little book about overdyeing and spot dyeing.

No conversation about color in hand-hooked rugs would be complete without discussing dyeing. We may delight in digging through a pile of as-is wool in search of just the right piece of wool to use in a hooked piece, but if we don't find it then what do we do?

You can, of course, buy pre-dyed, perfectly coordinated swatches that will fit into your color harmony, or hire someone to dye wools for you. I prefer a more hands-on approach. It's so satisfying to see those wonderful wool strips—in such gorgeous colors—drying on a line. Hanging the fabric outdoors is one of the pleasures of southern living.

Besides, it's fun to play with special dyeing techniques that give you many different color variations in a single piece of wool. I like to use braid, casserole, dip, salt shaker, and spot techniques, as well as overdyeing and stews.

The flower at right is part of a piece that I started in a hooking class, to study monochromatic color harmony in a rug. The piece is based on an eight-value swatch of bright green that begins with white.

I'm showing you this rug—and the wools used for the piece (see below)—so that you can see how wool dyed with special techniques can be used in a rug. Whether your color plan is based on a simple monochromatic color harmony or a far-reaching range of analogous colors, wool with varied color and texture adds much to your work. It's the use of all that we have available to us that gives us exciting rugs.

This pattern, called *Summer Romance*, was hooked with a color plan that's based on an ten-value white-to-green swatch. The addition of dip dyed wool and the salt shaker dyed wool was only the beginning of more variables. It is here we see the value of neutral gray wool. There's a dark gray I overdyed with green for the background and a medium gray wool dyed in three values in the medium-dark range. By the time I was satisfied, I had overdyed a plaid, a check, a black-and-white pincheck, a herringbone, and a tweed. Now I had the variety of color and texture to provide the interest necessary in this circle of flowers.

One of my favorite additions is a green dip dye on white wool, which is shown in the strips at left. The variations will give me a nice range for hooking motifs. Just like you'd find in nature, there will be several tints in the flowers and leaves . . . what a nice effect, especially for small flowers.

Here, at left, are some of the other pieces of wool that I dyed to create more interest and variety for my version of the *Summer Romance* pattern. I did a salt shaker dye to create the effect you can see on the bottom piece of wool in the photo. It, too, will add more interest to the piece.

A swatch is made up of several pieces of wool that have been dyed in a sequence of values in one or more colors. Three examples are shown in the photos on this page.

Often, the colors of each item in a swatch are different values of the same hue. In other words, dyeing starts with a single color. The wool changes value with the amount of dye that you use. You can also play with a dye to achieve a swatch that starts as one color and ends as another.

The most common swatches have six to eight values. I often encourage stretching the swatch to achieve more values. Seeing the results stretches your imagination because you'll be able to visualize even more beautiful color plans. The value swatches shown here go from light to dark and form a vertical path, as learned from the hue scale.

Six-value swatch Do you think I used different colors to come up with the beautiful array in the swatch shown at top left? I didn't. Every piece comes from a single dye color, which is PRO Chem #351 red, but I also used black dye with the red. All I did was vary the intensity of the color.

You're looking at a swatch that ranges from a gray-red to a higher intensity of red (a tone). This is a horizontal color path. (See page 22 for an explanation of color paths.)

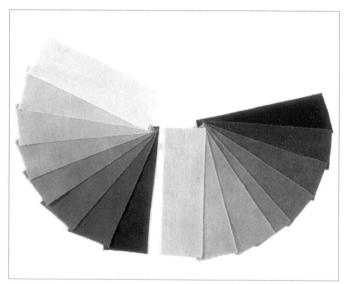

Eight-value swatch The photo at middle left shows a pair of eight-value swatches. Each represents a range of a single color, spanning from light to dark. This variation is along a vertical color path. (See page 21 for an explanation of a vertical color path.) The wide array that can be achieved is amazing, isn't it?

Joyce Krueger made both of these swatches for the color plan of her *Coventry* rug, which is shown on page 65. Of course, she didn't stop at just 16 values of these two colors for her beautiful rug. There are many, many more in the piece.

Ten-value swatch The photo at bottom left is interesting. It starts with one color, which looks like a soft apricot, a yellow-orange swatch, and ends with another that some would describe as mulberry, a red-purple. When a swatch changes from one color to another, it's called a transitional or transcolor swatch. Transitional swatches use two colors in graduated amounts that begin with one color and gradually transition to the second color. These types of swatches are created by dyeing colors along a diagonal color path from dark to light.

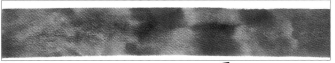

Braided Spot Dyeing *~immer* For braided spot dyeing, soak 1" strips of wool in vinegar water solution, squeeze water out, and simply braid three strips together. Place them in a flat pan with a very small amount of vinegar water. Spoon on one or more colors of dye solution (dry dye dissolved in water). You may need to turn the braid over and add dye to the backside. When the water clears, let it cool, then rinse, dry, and use wherever you want a spot dye. The multiple intensities and values make this a rich-looking piece of wool that's perfect for enlivening areas of a rug. I used a braided spot-dyed piece of wool for the tree in my *Bethlehem,* shown on page 44.

Casserole Dyeing As with the rest of the dye techniques, casserole dyeing will give you many color variations on your fabric, as shown above. The casserole technique is a transition of one color to another. Unlike the spot dye method, the colors in a piece of wool that's dyed with the casserole technique are blended together more closely. The color change is created by placing wet wool in a flat pan, applying the dyes, and then placing the pan into an oven to set the dye. Wool that has been dyed using the casserole technique has a striated effect because the dye is applied in sections and then pushed into each other with a spoon. When cut, the transition of color is very subtle. I love using pieces dyed this way for fields, hills, and leaves. The effect is especially striking in autumn colors.

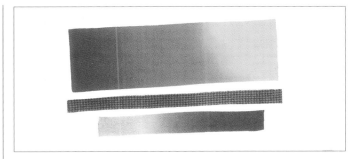

Dip Dyeing Compared to casserole dyeing, in dip dyeing the shift between colors is more gradual, and the colors are more even in a dip-dyed piece. You can see the result in the photo above. This happens because the wool isn't shaped before the dye is applied. You transition from one color to another on a single piece of material by dipping the wool into different dye solutions. The key to successful dip dyeing is keeping the fabric moving so that you don't get any lines in what should be an even gradation of color. The nice thing about this technique is that you can create dramatic color jumps, subtle gradations, or both effects in one piece. Your choices are broad.

Dip-dyed wool is excellent for shaded effects and scrolls. In fact, dip-dyed wool can replace fine shading.

Every experience deeply felt in life needs to be passed along whether it be through word or music, chiseled in stone, painted with a brush, sewn with a needle or "hooked into rug backing." It is a way of reaching for immortality—American Needlework

▶ **TIP** **Record Keeping**

At one time or another, almost all of us have cooked up our own special color, or tweaked a dye formula from one of our favorite books. When you do this, make sure that you write down what you did. You know that if you don't, you're certain to want that color again and might not be able to remember what you did. As a matter of habit, keep records of your dye formulas (with small swatches), any changes you made to a dye formula, and where you used it. I use small loose-leaf notebooks because they stack well on shelves. Use any tracking method that works for you, but do keep records.

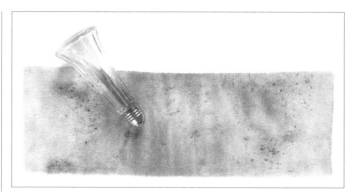

Overdying For every rug hooker, overdyeing is the most fascinating part of rug hooking. It's the ideal way to use up as-is wool in colors that you know you can't use. Simply dye these pieces to get unique and unusual new colors.

This technique yielded the wonderful wool that I used for the background of my *Antique Rose*, which is shown on page 64. The photo above shows the wool that I used—actually an old shirt—before and after overdyeing. Overdyeing cannot be an exact science, but if you go back to some color information learned early in life, you may have a reasonable idea of the colors you'll get from overdyeing wools.

- Red over yellow gives colors between red and yellow on the color circle.
- Red over blue gives the colors between red and blue on the color scale.
- Yellow over blue gives colors between yellow and blue on the color circle.
- Overdyeing opposites on the color circle makes the color brown.
- On the Artist's Color Wheel, try the color with the black over it to see the color that really ends up gray.
- Look at the last two outer sections of the colored tips on the color star to see color with gray.

Salt Shaker Dyeing Like all of the other dye methods discussed in this section, the name of this one also describes the process. Simply put, you mix dye with salt, and shake the concoction on to wet wool. The wool is first placed in a water and vinegar bath, and then the dry mix is shaken over the surface. Most dyes today are blended, so the dye will break down into other colors to give you the wonderful variables.

The wool piece shown above was colored with a bright green dye. When the dye and salt hit the water and blend, purple and blue emerged and spread across the fabric.

The secret to successful salt shaker dyeing is leaving the wool alone in the dye bath. Don't stir it up after sprinkling the dye and salt mixture onto the surface. Use very little water in a flat pan and remember to watch the pan so it doesn't cook dry.

I use salt shaker dyed wool in small areas where I want a spotted effect that is on a smaller scale than I could achieve with a spot dye.

There is no one way of seeing a thing no matter how simple that thing may be. Its planes, values, colors—all its characteristics are, as it were, shifted before us as we first see and it is up to us to arrange them according to our understanding.

—Author Unknown

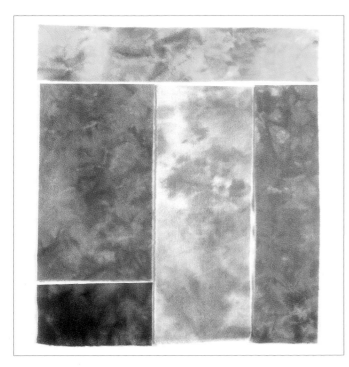

Spot Dyeing For this technique, up to four dye colors are placed on wool that's scrunched into a flat pan. Spot dyeing achieves an excellent range of colors. You can work with colors that are closely related or are distinctly different. Spotted wools give a sense of movement, as our eye moves from color to color in one piece of wool. The photo above shows the versatility of this method. The wool pieces range from subtle to dramatic.

Stew Dyeing Just stack your wools and get cooking. The idea is to use an assortment of wools. Add a few pinches of Tide without bleach, fill the pot with water and cook them togeth-

er so that the colors bleed and marry. I try to insert wool pieces that I know bleed a lot. If you don't have a "bleeder," use a dye formula.

I always put a 16" x 12" piece of white wool on top of every stew. This is a wonderful way to build a collection of off-white wool. When you decide the wools have changed color to your liking, add two or three glugs of vinegar to the pot and simmer a little longer until the water is clear.

All of the wool shown at lower left came from a single stew with the smaller pieces at the top showing the original color of wool. Unlike the stew you eat, do not stir the pot.

The gorgeous arrangement of swatches above are the colors that I worked into my rug called *Oyster Bay Antique*, which is shown in the Gallery, on page 58. The wool shown here was created with a stew, so that I'd have just the right colors to hook the baskets. To get the results you see, I used the assortment of wool seen in the small fan—dark gray, medium gray, blue-gray, textured gray, gray check, camel, beige, and white. When I made the rug I also added light yellow and pink on top.

I used a dark brown wool as a bleeder for the original stew. Since I no longer have that wool, I now mix $1/4$ teaspoon of black dye and $1/2$ teaspoon of brown dye. Dissolve in hot water. Fill a large pot with water and add the dye solution and stir well. Add the wool in the sequence shown. When it begins to simmer, glug vinegar around the edge of the pot and squish the wool down to move the vinegar into the wool. Simmer until the water clears.

I was determined to create just the right colors for the antique look and I did a lot of dying to come up with the right effect. It wasn't until I saw the results of my stew, which was a last resort, that I was satisfied.

CHAPTER THREE

Developing Color Harmonies

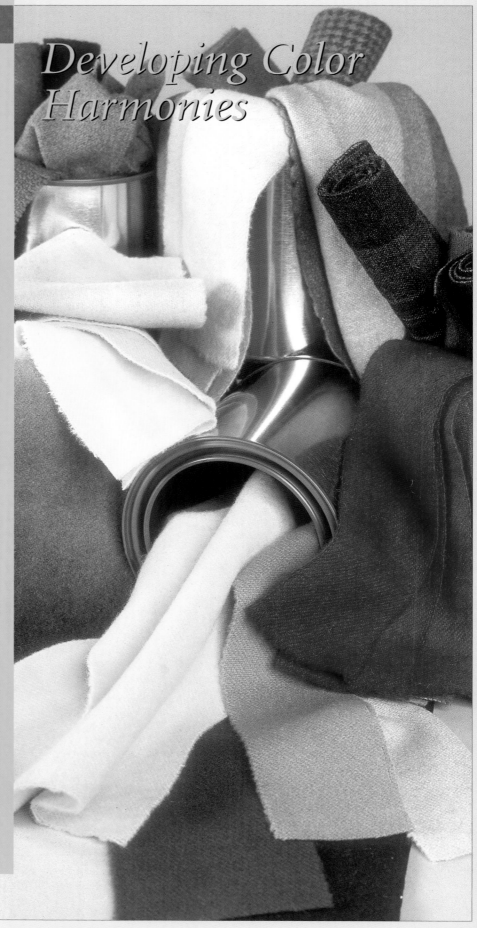

Every form of color is beautiful. The challenge is to decide what form to use, in what quantity, and in what combination.

A harmony is a pleasing combination of colors. There are, of course, many types of harmonies, but most are based on the work of color pioneer Michel Eugene Chevrèul. In his book The Principles of Harmony and Contrast of Colours, *he introduced a way to group colors so that they'd engage the audience. His system imposes structure, interest, and order.*

The system is based on harmonies, which group together pleasing colors. These harmonies are called monochromatic, complementary, tetradic, analogous, and triadic. The arrangements are so successful that they've been taught and used in art education in the entire Western world and are still used extensively today.

After you have chosen one— maybe two—colors for your rug, use these harmonies to help choose the remaining hues for your color plan.

In 2003, students in my class in South Carolina learned about color harmonies by hooking a pattern called Bethlehem, designed by Jane McGown Flynn. They each chose a harmony and went to work, using as much as-is wool as possible. They worked with #3- or #4-cut wool, or a combination of both.

Bethlehem, 10" in diameter, #3-and 4-cut wool on burlap. Designed by Jane McGown Flynn. Hooked by Betty Krull, Greer, South Carolina, 2004.

This harmony is any one hue, used in a number of shades, tints, and tones. You might think this is limiting in a hooked piece, but it's not. Remember, there were 46 colors on the hue scale shown on page 20, all derived from one color, with gray or white added.

The greater the difference in values and intensities in your wools, the more dramatic the effect in the finished piece. If you use closer intensities and values, you'll end up with a more subdued effect. Contrast is necessary in monochromatic color harmonies, so try including some black.

When my students were developing their color plans for the *Bethlehem* designs, I decided to take another look at the monochromatic harmony. The result is shown above.

The color star on page 30 shows the monochromatic harmony that I used for my rug. I chose red because it is my favorite color.

A monochromatic harmony may be more interesting when you use it with a color that isn't a primary. Although red is a primary, I found it easy to use.

I also wanted to play with gray and black, to explore how they that can be used to add interest without breaking a color harmony. (Black, gray, and white can be added to any harmony.) With the hooked piece on this page, I used color theory as my tool and then let my imagination guide me to interesting placement of gray.

▶ **TIP Path to Success**

To make a rug with a monochromatic color harmony, choose one color or a single dye formula. With this decision made, you can then play with the values and intensities. Some of the most interesting effects are accomplished by overdyeing gray-and-white wools with your color and adding black.

The photo above uses monochromatic red colors—with just 5 values from a vertical color path plus a spot dye and dip dye.

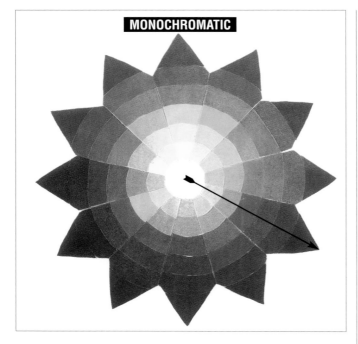

MONOCHROMATIC

The secret to a successful monochromatic color plan is the use of one color and contrast. This color star shows the range of variables that I used for my monochromatic piece. If you want to explore a color plan that's based on one color, your starting point can be any hue on this star. For more interest, concentrate on contrast: light, medium, and dark versions of the hue. Don't forget to add values for even more variety.

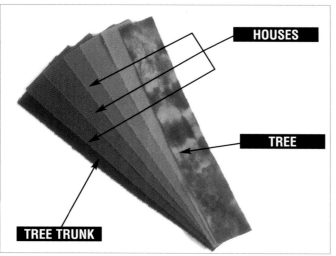

HOUSES

TREE

TREE TRUNK

My hooked piece on page 29 was worked with wool from the same swatch that's shown at left.

The color plan began with small amounts of red that were the remainders of a swatch purchased from the Dorr Mill Store. This is a six-value swatch and I used values #3, 4, and 5 for the houses, to which I added the darkest value (#6) for the tree trunks.

I used PRO Chem red #351 and black #672 for the spot dye wool. Can you see the purple? This color appears when you make a spot dye with red and black. This spot dyed wool added character to the trees without introducing textured wool. The red and black in the spot dye creates movement, which counteracts the flatness of the other wool colors.

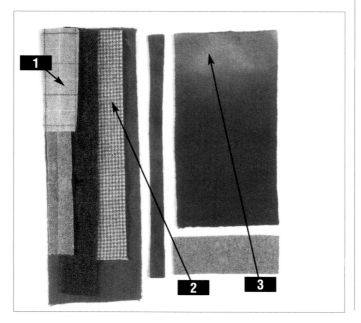

1

2   3

The textured pieces shown among the wools at left were used for the fields. Wool #1, the windowpane plaid with lines of red and black, is in two of the fields. Hooked into the piece, the black and red lines in the plaid pop out, adding a bit of fun and interest. I hooked a very small-scale, houndstooth check, (wool #2) into the bottom field. I opted against a large-scale check because more white would have been visible. I wanted the field to look gray. The four solid gray wools shown in the photo were used in several ways. The lighter gray is in the lower fields, the medium-dark gray colors are on each side of the houses, and the charcoal gray is in the large hill. A very undistinguished black-and-white tweed created texture in one hill.

I wanted a light horizon line against the dark hill, which is where the dip-dyed wool (#3) came into play. One end of the wool is light red while the other end is charcoal gray. I dyed additional charcoal gray wool for the upper sky. All of the sky colors were dyed over plain white wool.

As you develop a monochromatic harmony, it's important to keep in mind that you can overdye your wools for more color variety. For my version of *Bethlehem*, I wanted to see what I had in gray as-is wool that would give me variables I could use to hook the gray hills. But I wanted to go further: In the photo at right you can see how I applied color to some of the same grays shown in the photo on page 30. The photo on this page shows gray and white wools overdyed with red. From left to right on the fan, there's a gray plaid (wool #1 in the previous photo), a light gray wool, a black-and-white mini tweed, white, and a gray and white houndstooth check (wool #3 in the previous photo). This is a reminder about the value of gray wools, for use as is or over-dyed to suit your color harmony.

As you can see in the photo on page 29, the star is hooked with a silver metallic braid. There wasn't any theory behind my choice. Silver just felt right, and it's a nice contrast to all of the gray in the rug. Personal preference is important. As I often say, unless you're making a rug for someone else, this is your piece. Your personality and preferences should come through. All the stars in the *Bethlehem* designs are hooked with metallic braid. The silver in this one is in keeping with the grays used here. However, gold braid would not necessarily be part of any color harmonies. It was a choice that adds much interest.

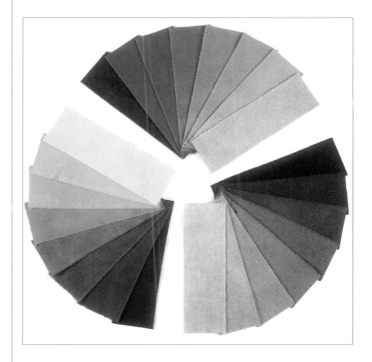

Monochromatic Dye Pot

Here are some ways that you can use dyes and dyeing techniques to add variety and interest to a monochromatic color harmony.

- Use black, neutral gray, or white as-is, or overdye the wool with your monochromatic color choice.
- Spot dye white wool with black and a color.
- Dye the wool with a salt shaker technique.
- Add interest with textured wool.

▶ TIP Monochromatic Color

Monochromatic color harmonies can be made from any color on the color star. Go back and look at Sharon Richmond's *Southwest III* on page 6, and her use of blue-green. Envision a monochromatic harmony in any of the 3 colors in the above swatches—consider the challenge of orange (the "brown" swatch).

Bethlehem, 10" in diameter, #3-cut wool on burlap. Designed by Jane McGown Flynn. Hooked by Juanita Baker, Fletcher, North Carolina, 2003.

Complementary harmony is any two colors that are directly opposite one another on the color star. A rug worked in this scheme has more contrast and more stability than any other color harmony. Chemist and color expert Michel Eugene Chevreul liked this arrangement more than any other: "The contrast of opposite colors is most agreeable. The complementary assortment is superior to every other."

I agree with Chevreul on many things, but not this time . . . my favorite harmony has to be the triad, which is explained on page 42.

For a complementary color plan, you can use values and intensities of both colors from a diagonal, horizontal, or vertical path.

A complementary harmony can be visually shocking or compelling or, when used with restraint, interesting and exciting. Proportion is critical. You need to use unequal color areas and unequal values and intensities. In other words, make one color the star of your rug and let the second color play a supporting role. Usually, the higher intensity color is the best choice for the dominant color.

Rug hooker Juanita Baker of Fletcher, North Carolina, did a great job exploring the cool and warm sides of purple and yellow in her interpretation of Jane McGown Flynn's *Bethlehem* pattern above.

▶ TIP Heavy Metal

Using metallic braid, which is sold in packages at craft stores, isn't difficult. It does, however, take some patience. Make sure you pull the ends of the braid to the back of pattern, not to the top as we normally do when we're hooking. Don't trim the ends too closely to the backing. I like to put a dab of white glue on each end to prevent it from fraying.

Pick any color on a star or wheel, draw a line through it and across to the other side, and you have its opposite, or complementary, color. That's how simple it is to pick this scheme. The most important thing to remember about this harmony is the effect the colors have on one another. Using opposite colors creates a visually dramatic effect because one color intensifies its opposite when they are used in different values and intensities.

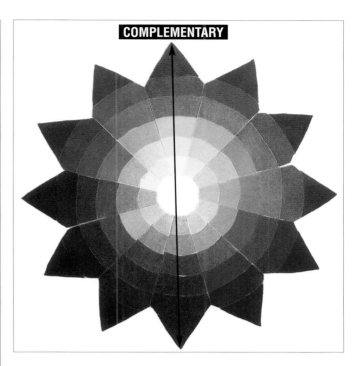

Juanita used 7 values of purple which covered a range from tints to a shade. The shade is used for the range of hills and the tint of purple provides a light contrast at the horizon line. She used a mid-value of purple for a small hill. She gradually increased the depth of the color ending with tones of purple at the top. Adding interest are the horizontal hooking lines that she has used for a dramatic effect of the sky.

The photo at left shows several complementary color harmonies. The complement of a primary color is always a secondary color. This primary-secondary combination is easy to work with.

The complement of a tertiary, or hybrid, color is another tertiary color. In other words, you'd be working with combinations of yellow-orange, red-orange, red-purple, purple-blue, blue-green, and yellow-green.

Tertiary complementary harmonies can be dramatic, shocking, or theatrical. For this reason, you need more thought and planning when using these color schemes in your hooked pieces.

Complementary Dye Pot

There are lots of fun dyes and dyeing techniques that you can apply to wool when you want to add variety to a complementary color harmony.

- Spot dye a swatch with values of one color. Don't combine two complementary colors. You'll end up with a muddy gray-brown.
- Try a casserole dye, but do so with great caution so you don't end up with gray-brown where the colors meet.
- Include a variety of textures. Be cautious about using plaids that contain only the two complements, such as red and green. They may hook into your rug as brown.
- Overdye gray, particularly a check or plaid, in one or both of the colors. This will give you added interest and deeper values.
- Add black to the color palette for a touch of sophistication.

"Creativity requires fluency—lots of ideas; flexibility—lots of variety; originality—your own; elaboration—the details."—Author Unknown

Betty's Petticoat, 47 ¹/₂ x 11 ¹/₂", #3-cut wool on monk's cloth. Designed and hooked by Joyce Krueger, Waukesha, Wisconsin, 2003.

This color harmony uses one key color combined with two others that lay next to its exact opposite on the color star or wheel. In other words, it uses three colors: any hue desired, plus the two that are beside its complement.

In the rug above, for example, the key color is blue-green. Its complement is red-orange, so orange and red complete the rug's color harmony. This can be confusing, but looking at a color star or wheel can help you sort this out. You can see the specific harmony for *Betty's Petticoat* marked on the color star at right.

Betty's Petticoat was designed and hooked by Joyce Krueger of Waukesha, Wisconsin, in 2003. Three women named Betty were involved in designing, color planning, and hooking the piece. To learn more about this rug, see the commentary on page 63.

To develop a color plan with this harmony, begin with one color that will be dominant in the finished rug. This doesn't mean that the color has to be used more than the other two. Instead, it can simply be the strongest color. As you decide which colors to apply to different elements in your pattern, think about using unequal amounts of both complements, with much variation in intensities and values. I like to use one or two color paths, be they diagonal, horizontal, or vertical.

In *Betty's Petticoat,* shown above, one color is blue-green. The complement is red-orange, so blue-green, orange, and red complete the rug's color harmony. You can see this arrangement in the color star.

▶**TIP** **Learn From Others**

Take advantage of the wide variety of teachers available. Learn from all of them. You will find such a wealth of ideas and information from each one. Use what works for you to increase your skills and expand your horizons. If you go to rug school do not take lessons with your home teacher. Try someone new.

Split Complementary Dye Pot

Want more variety in the split complementary color plan for your rug? Here are some suitable dyeing techniques that you might want to consider.

- Dye individual swatches using any or all three colors.
- Dip dye by applying one color to each end of the swatch, or use any combination of two colors.
- Try a casserole dye using all three colors.
- Overdye natural, gray, or white wool textures with any of the colors in the harmony.

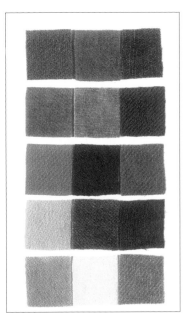

As the wool samples at left show, there are many beautiful color schemes to be explored in this harmony. Split complementary color harmonies are very easy to work with and have great visual appeal. Do any of the colors remind you of flowers? I frequently use split-complementary color plans as a launching point for elements in my rugs. This is inevitable because I love hooking flowers, and the harmony is excellent for floral designs.

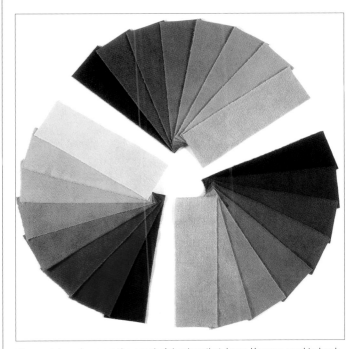

The swatches above are the wonderful colors that Joyce Krueger used to hook *Betty's Petticoat,* on page 34. This is a classic split complementary color harmony.

Bethlehem, 10" in diameter, #3-cut wool on burlap. Designed by Jane McGown Flynn. Hooked by Barbara Luke, Greer, South Carolina, 2003. Barbara based her *Bethlehem* color plan on a double complement. She chose red and green plus blue and orange. She picked this color scheme after admiring Marilyn Denning's version of the *Coventry* rug pattern, which you can see on page 69.

The concept behind this harmony is similar to the split complementary scheme, except that more colors are involved. This is a harmony of four, because the double complement uses two pairs of complements. In other words, there's one key color, its exact opposite, plus one other set of complements from any place on the color star. The combination red and green, plus blue and orange are a good example of this harmony.

Note that red and green are one of the pairs in the example and in Barbara's hooked piece. Yet the second pair isn't the same in both instances. Complementary color pairs don't have to be equally spaced from one other.

In a rug color plan, a successful double complement relies on many values and intensities of four colors. By using two sets of complementary hues, your color plan will have the potential for a very harmonious blend of colors. (Interestingly, this harmony is often referred to as a discordant theme.) Start with a key color that'll be dominant. It can be the color that you'll use most, worked in a variety of values and intensities, or it can be the most intense color, used in lesser amounts. As with the other harmonies, you can pick the desired intensities and values from a diagonal, horizontal, or vertical color path.

Double Complementary Dye Pot

Adding variety to a double complementary harmony is a simple matter using any of the following dyeing techniques.

- Use value swatches.
- Dip dye using one or two colors or a single color.
- Make a casserole dye using three or four colors.
- Overdye grays with any color in the harmony for deeper colors.

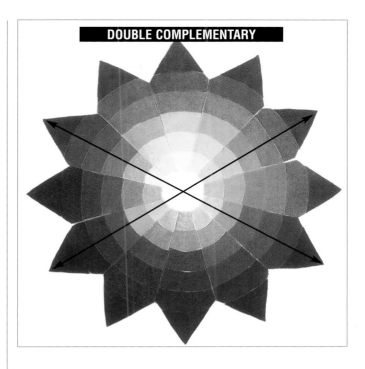

Barbara's *Bethlehem* was worked with a 12-value swatch, shown above. We call this a transitional, or transcolor, swatch because it starts in one color and ends with its complement. To do this, the colors travel a diagonal path on the hue scale. You'll always get a muddy color when you combine complementary colors, so it stands to reason that you end up with a brown-green at the center of this swatch.

This transitional swatch goes from blue to orange. Barbara and I added two blue values on one end and two orange values on the other end.

Prisms #7, called Country Pumpkin, was the original formula. We changed PRO Chem turquoise #478 to PRO Chem blue #490.

Barbara added more blue wool, in darker values, for the sky. A variety of orange wools were used in the fields, hills, and houses. The brown-green is also used for fields, hills, and trees. Red, which completes the double complementary color harmony, adds spark to the piece.

With the closely related colors that we find in a transitional swatch, we need to make sure that light and dark values of the swatch contrast with each other.

Each of us is born with a capacity for growth—
not just physical growth, but growth of the ability
to think, to create works of beauty, to live freely
and wonderously and add to the lives of others
—Adlai Stevenson

Fast and Fun

I highly recommend the *Bethlehem* pattern, designed by Jane McGown Flynn, to any hooker who wants to learn about color. This pattern is excellent because it's small, can be personalized, doesn't require a lot of wool, and hooks up quickly. Let's use this pattern to consider some alternative split-complementary harmonies for color plans.

Why not try yellow-green, red, and purple? Try several dark values of purple for the sky and pink (light values of red) for the houses. This makes it possible to use dark values of yellow-green for the hills. Make sure the values used for the hills contrast with the purple in the sky. A yellow-green plaid would be excellent, or you could substitute a wool that has been spot dyed with yellow-green and purple. Use lighter values of yellow-green for the fields. Make certain you have variety in textures and values. Use a very dark value of red for the tree trunk. You might want to consider a red-and-black spot dye for the trees.

For another split complementary concept, make a spot dye with several values of orange. This will give you a dramatic sunset sky. Blue-purple would make wonderful hills, and the fields can all be hooked in varying values of blue-green. Make sure you add some textures. Use a very dark orange (brown) for the tree trunks. Consider a blue-green plaid, created by overdying gray plaid, for the tops of the trees.

Bethlehem, 10" in diameter, #3-cut wool on burlap. Designed by Jane McGown Flynn. Hooked by Linda Johnstone, Greenville, South Carolina, 2003.

As the name suggests, this harmony is based on four hues. The ones you select should be evenly spaced around the color star. You can choose a mix of primary, secondary, and tertiary hues. You can use a rectangle or a square to determine the four colors. When you use the rectangle, there's always one color between corners on each short side of the rectangle and three colors between the corners on the long sides of the rectangle. If you use a square, there will be two colors between the corner colors on each side. Where the corners end are the colors you'll use.

I find it difficult to visualize a tetradic harmony. It's hard to determine because you have to make a rectangle across the star, then skip one color, or make a square and skip two colors. I draw the choices directly on a copy of a color star, to make sure I get it right.

For the *Bethlehem* piece above, Linda Johnstone of Greenville, South Carolina, chose blue-green, blue-violet, red-orange, and yellow-orange. She didn't use all of the colors equally. It's not the amount of color that matters. Rather, it's the way that it can be used to break up another color. In Linda's piece there are only tiny bits of red-orange, which you can see floating through the field at the bottom of the pattern. Red-orange is the highest intensity color in the rug. So, by using the red-orange in the foreground, the viewer's eye is drawn forward.

Another of my students, Kay Davis, also hooked her *Bethlehem* with a tetradic color harmony. (See the photo on page 39). Her interpretation is based on the more primary combination of green, purple, red, and yellow. Kay picked a bright purple for the sky. She got a lot of hooking in before realizing that it didn't work. To make her piece more appealing, she had to reverse-hook (pull out loops), and then work the area with a darker purple.

In addition to choosing a color in a harmony, it's important to also consider the value of the color.

Everyone reworks portions of almost every rug they hook. In Kay's case, she carefully chose the colors. The swatches looked great in our hands. It wasn't until Kay worked on the sky that the problem emerged. This does happen, so don't beat yourself up if you find yourself in a similar situation.

Bethlehem, 10" in diameter, #3-cut wool on burlap. Designed by Jane McGown Flynn. Hooked by Kay Davis, Greenville, South Carolina, 2003. The tetrad, like the double complement, is a four-color harmony. For the *Bethlehem* shown on this page, Linda placed a rectangle over a color star. The hue in each corner—blue-green, blue-purple, red-orange, and yellow-orange—became the colors for her rug. This star shows the color choices in her harmony.

▶TIP **Keep a Nail File**

Keep a nail file, Band-aids and hand lotion with your rug hooking tools—they may be just as necessary as your hook and scissors. Try to use a hand lotion with lanolin, an ingredient in sheep wool.

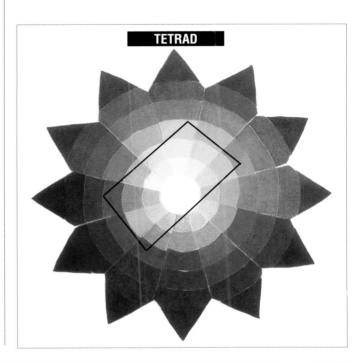

TETRAD

It's Only Natural

TULIP

FOXGLOVE

ROSE OF SHARON

I'm an avid flower gardener, and I plant my garden by color. I delight in hooking flowers, especially white flowers. The tulip is hooked with a dip-dyed wool, dipping just a tiny edge of the red at the edge of the wool. I hooked the edges

in a comma shape to give the ruffled effect. The Rose of Sharon has purple veins radiating from a green and purple center. The veins are hooked with a #2-cut, the flower with a #6. Foxgloves have a yellow green throat with red-purple spots.

Since I've hooked this rug, the flower world has produced an abundance of yellow green plants for gardens—I love that!

Bethlehem, 10" in diameter, #3-cut wool on burlap. Designed by Jane McGown Flynn. Hooked by Kathy Forbes, Simpsonville, South Carolina, 2003.

You can see the analogous harmony in a rainbow. This scheme is easy to understand because it's little more than several colors that are side-by-side on the color star or wheel.

There are many opinions about the number of colors that can be used in an analogous color harmony. There are experts who say that four hues work best, but why not three, five, or six? Some definitions of the analogous harmony would limit us to any three colors that are side by side on the color star. I think the choice is yours.

We instinctively understand the analogous harmony because it's a collection of natural colors that we see everywhere in nature. Think about water. People describe it as purple, blue-purple, blue, blue-green, or green. That's a range of colors found side-by-side on the color star. And you can find an analogous harmony within a single natural element, like a rose; the petals may shade from red to red-orange, with red-purple in the deep center.

It's easy to get pleasing results with an analogous harmo-

ny because the colors enhance one another and the shifts are subtle gradations, especially on the cool side of the color star. A rug plan based on this arrangement is best when it includes only one primary.

The color plan in Kathy Forbes' design, above, is analogous. Nothing stands out . . . yet everything stands out. You can identify each color, but your eyes never stop at any one of them. Instead, they move from color to color.

▶ **TIP Less Is More**

Despite our comfort with the natural colors in the analogous harmony, this scheme requires careful thought to be successful. Your goal should be to create a feeling of unity even though you're using so many intensities and values. If this color harmony is new to you, then it may be best to limit yourself to a color plan of four hues.

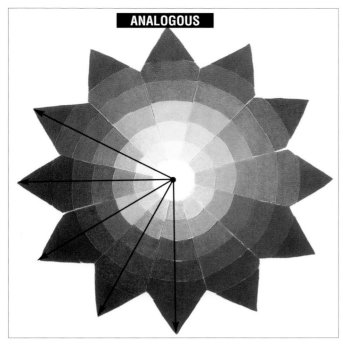

ANALOGOUS

This star indicates the analogous color harmony that Kathy Forbes used for her rug on page 40. It features purple, blue-purple, blue, blue-green, and green. The houses aren't hooked in a high intensity blue, yet they're noticed because Kathy has surrounded them with colors that enhance them. The light values of blue-green in the fields next to the houses and the mid-value greens in the hills make a frame for the houses. The light green tree is almost like a reflection of the star.

The blue in the sky pulls your eye up from the houses. Kathy mixed the blues and purple colors together. These colors are so closely related that the combination gives this part of the work a sense of movement. I love the sky, because the little diagonal lines of blue wool create an iridescent effect.

Looking at the pattern above, you can see the tremendous variety that's available in an analogous harmony. Juanita Baker hooked in light, very light, dark, dull, and bright (not too bright) colors. It all comes down to lights and darks, which are intensities and values.

Juanita was determined to begin with a very dark blue-purple for a midnight sky. This was her starting point. From there, she branched out to purple, red-purple, red, and red-orange. The houses are very spotty gray and red-purple wool. In the foreground, there's one tiny piece of wool that has a gold thread running through it. This adds quiet drama to the piece.

Analogous Dye Pot

A rug with an analogous color harmony relies heavily on dyeing techniques. Here are some suggestions to help you introduce a wide range of intensities and values to your work.

- Use only one primary color; play with a range between the next primary on the color star.
- Introduce swatches in closely related values, to ease transitions between colors.
- Spot dye using two or three colors.
- Dip dye wool so that there's one color on one end and another color at the other end
- Feature three colors that are neighbors on the color star in a casserole dye.
- Overdye several colors of wool with one dye formula, to create some closely related colors.

The color wheel at left shows the colors that Juanita used to hook her interpretation of the *Bethlehem* pattern, which is shown above right. The piece features four colors. Because they're beside one another on the color star, this is an analogous color harmony. This type of harmony isn't limited to four colors. You can choose two, three, four . . . or even more colors for your analogous harmony.

ANALOGOUS

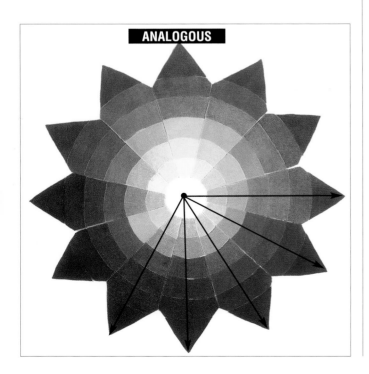

Bethlehem, 10" in diameter, #3-cut wool on burlap. Designed by Jane McGown Flynn. Hooked by Mildred Young, Greenville, South Carolina, 2003.

Any three colors that are equidistant on the color star make up a triadic harmony. This is my favorite scheme. I use the red, blue, and yellow combination to decorate my home because it's effective with my eclectic decorating style. The color harmony also works well with antiques.

The blue-green, yellow-orange, and red-purple triad that Mildred Young hooked for the *Bethlehem* rug, above, was a big stretch for her. This is a difficult blend of colors, and Mildred managed to pull it off artfully.

The buildings are variations of red-purple, which contrasts nicely with the yellow-orange fields and hills. One section of the sky is blue-green, and then the rest of the sky shifts to blue hues. This happened because we were using scrap wool for this project. We didn't have any blue-green pieces that worked, so she found blue colors that made an easy transition from the blue-green to the blue. Mildred decided to move out of the color harmony and choose other hues.

I think it's important that you have the freedom to choose colors that are outside a color harmony. The harmony is only the starting point.

Some triadic color harmonies give a rug a strong theme, such as oriental or primitive. Overall, Mildred's rug colors have an oriental feeling.

Look! Look! Look! I've learned that the more creative you are the more things you notice.—From "Live, Learn and Pass It On" by H. Jackson Brown

The color scheme marked on this star was the starting point for Mildred Young's rug, shown on page 42. Mildred was thrilled to be exploring the triadic color harmony. Being able to learn something different and work with new colors can be an exciting happening. It's interesting to see the number of different values of colors there are in Mildred's little piece. There are five values of red-purple, six of yellow-orange, one of blue-green, and four of blue. This proves that it's the variety of intensities and values that make this a wonderful hooked piece.

TRIADIC COLOR HARMONY

The red, blue, and yellow triad (see the wool swatches at left) is primitive, direct, and unsophisticated. It has unusual charm when hooked into simple designs. To achieve the primitive effect in a rug, use a variety of fabrics such as recycled, as-is wool, textures, and stews. Also consider overdyeing checks and plaids for even more variety, and include many of color values. Use unequal amounts of the colors, and make sure they are relatively pure (have strong-to moderate-chroma).

The red, yellow, and blue triad can also be used for oriental designs. The key to this effect is using traditional oriental colors such as rich reds, blues, golds, and dirty whites. Use value swatches, spot dyes, and dip dyes for interest.

Yellow-orange, blue-green, and red-purple also have an oriental quality and keep fabrics more refined. I like smooth flannels. Use value swatches, transcolors, casserole dyes, and spot dyes for interest.

The example shown at right has an oriental feeling to it because I hooked with yellow-orange, blue-green, and red-purple. Compare the colors in this piece to Mildred Youngs' *Bethlehem*—different values, different designs, different effect. This is my own design, which I hooked on an unknown backing with wool scraps, back in 2000. This little piece was hooked because I needed a visual aid for a display board that I use for teaching The Color Course.

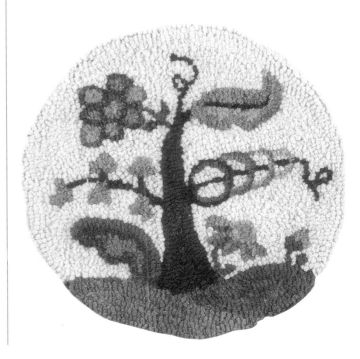

The triad marked on the color wheel at left represents the colors used in the photo below. As previously explained, the harmony is a triad because there are three colors, and they're spaced an equal distance from one another on the color star. The three colors are all considered secondary colors. They're so-named because each one is made by combining two primary colors.

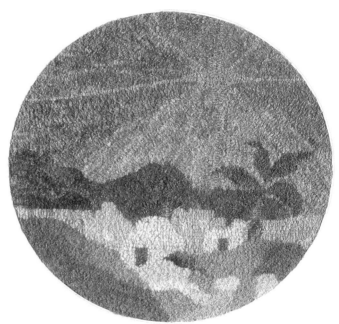

I hooked this version of the *Bethlehem* pattern, at right, when I developed the color course. It's a triad of red-orange, blue-purple, and yellow-green. I added some gray for the doors and windows because black, gray, and white can be added to any color harmony. The star is hooked with a wool that has a metallic overlay, somewhat like a double-faced wool. The metallic effects in all of the other *Bethlehem* pieces were made with gold or silver braid that we bought in the notions department at fabric stores.

It's Only Natural

I never discourage my students from playing with color. It's very important to me that they stretch their ability to use color effectively.

Marion O'Beirne started her color plan for the *Bethlehem* pattern shown here by choosing two colors. In this case they were green and yellow-green. Then she decided to develop an analogous color harmony. This meant that she could expand her color plan to include yellow, yellow-orange, orange, and red-orange.

This is a huge range of colors, and not always the approach I recommend for an analogous scheme. Yet Marion made this color plan work. The sky is great—very dramatic. I expect an angel to pop out.

Triadic Combinations

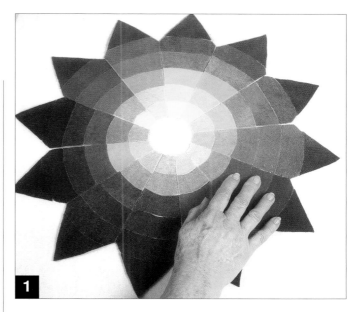

For most color harmonies, we use diagonal, horizontal, or vertical color paths. The three colors for a triad, on the other hand, are picked from a circular color path.

After you choose the three colors for your triad, you need to determine which color will be dominant in your color plan, which color will be secondary, and which color will be used in much smaller amounts.

Triadic variations aren't complex, but there is a handy trick for determining a pleasing balance of these three colors for your rug. By simply tracing a comma shape around the star, you can see where the intensities and values are that you should try using. While this may sound strange, it really works.

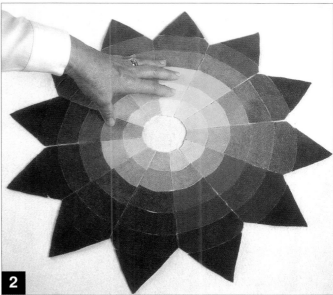

1 Start the comma at the triadic color you want to use the most. Place three fingers on the red portion of the color star. The values that your fingers touch are the ones that you'll use in your rug's harmony. Are they in the middle, dark end, or the lightest section? Note which values you want to use. This example shows a red, blue, and yellow triad. Since the red will be dominant, on the color star I placed my fingers at the beginning of the comma, on red. (Because my color star is very large, I used four fingers rather than three. If you're using the color star pullout in the center of this book, use only three fingers.).

2 Using a circular path, slide your hand to the second color. In the example, my hand shifted over to yellow. My hand has moved slightly toward the interior of the star, because I'm tracing a comma shape. Using only two fingers as your measurement, determine where your colors are coming from in the yellow. Note your choices. Again, I'm using three fingers in the example because the color star is so large. You should use two.

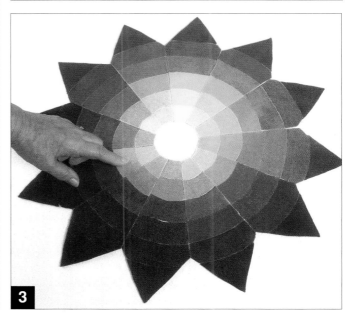

3 Continue tracing around the star in a comma shape until you reach the third color. Place only one finger (two fingers in my case) on the color that'll be the smallest amount in your color plan. The position of your finger shows whether you'll be using a dark, medium, or light value.

CHAPTER FOUR

Planning a Rug

It's time to put the color theory in this book to work. In this chapter, you'll learn how to pick colors for a specific rug. It starts with detailed photos and step-by-step instructions, using one of my rugs as an example. The last part of the chapter presents the theory behind color planning, to address any remaining situations that you might encounter.

One of my goals in The Secrets of Color in Hand-Hooked Rugs is to help you understand that color planning is a journey. You'll see that even an expert who lives and breathes color will rework an area to get a rug just right.

Color plans don't spring completely formed from my head. I may have an idea where I'm going, but after I've chosen my wool and started hooking, I may discover that some selections aren't successful. So I'm going to show you my starting point, explain my decisions, and even show you color choices that didn't work out. You'll learn by watching me work.

My goal is to help you develop the skills and knowledge to create your own special rugs . . . and make fearless color decisions.

Lamb's Tongues and Sunflowers, 27" x 21", #5- and 3-cut wool on rug warp. Designed by Pris Buttler. Hooked by Betty Krull, Greer, South Carolina, 2004.

This little rug, called *Lamb's Tongues and Sunflowers* by Pris Buttler looks simple, but it isn't. The field, hills, lamb's tongue border, and trees, were all carefully color planned for interest, texture, and variety.

A nearly empty field in the lower left-hand corner needed an interesting treatment. A large field above the sunflowers, on the right, called for varied color so that it didn't look flat. And, for more interest, I added a path to split the bottom half of the pattern.

The hills and tree require careful color selection so that each shape would be distinct. Finally, it can be difficult to choose the best colors for lamb's tongues.

The finished piece, is hooked mostly with #5-cut wool. (I used #3-cut wool for small details like the flowers, a fence, a rooster, and a tin of marigolds.)

On the following pages, you'll see how I tackled the challenges of this rug, as well as learn how to apply the color planning process to your own pieces.

My rug is based on a split complementary color harmony consisting of yellow, orange, and purple-blue. Yellow is the dominant color: it's the strongest, and also the one that I used the most. Yellow is used in many intensities in this piece. There are varying shades of yellow for sunflowers, and dark values of yellow (which we call green) and/or orange for the hills and some of the fields.

The photos that accompany the steps on the following pages show the hooked elements of the rug as I discuss the

As you examine your pattern, take a critical look at each element that makes up the design. Then ask yourself a series of questions: How do I want to interpret the pattern? How will I personalize it? Will I make design changes? What's my game plan?

planning process and the colors that I chose. Keep in mind that I usually plan all of the colors before I start hooking. I almost always debate a few parts as I hook . . . and I always remain open to change.

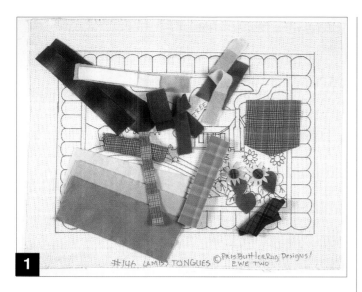

1 Decide where the piece will be used. Although I hooked *Lamb's Tongues* and *Sunflowers* specifically for *The Secrets of Color in Hand-Hooked Rugs*, I plan to use this piece as part of a vignette in my home. The props include an antique school desk and chair, as well as some old rug hooking books. The colors in my rug need to work with these home accessories. The house in *Lamb's Tongues and Sunflowers* reminds me of the buildings that are typical of the lowlands of South Carolina, the state where I live. I have three pen-and-ink and watercolor paintings that depict the same kind of buildings, so I used these as inspiration. As you get started, collect visual aids like fabric, paint, and wallpaper samples. Use art books, garden catalogs, greeting cards, and gift-wrap paper. If you don't have a file or box full of ideas, now is a good time to start one.

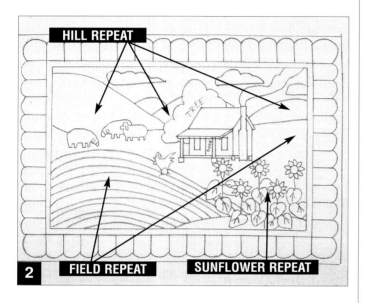

2 Analyze the pattern, looking carefully at each element. This is the time to decide if you'll make design changes for a personal interpretation of the piece. You'll also choose your first one or two colors.

Remember to look for repeats in the design. In *Lamb's Tongues and Sunflowers*, the fields, hills, and sunflowers are repeats because there's more than one of each item. I consider all of the sunflowers to be one design element. At this time, I also start choosing colors. Sunflower colors were easy to select. Because they're over-scale, and I hooked them in yellow—a high intensity color—the sunflowers became the rug's focal point. Although the pattern contains large fields and hills, the house is the second most important element. Using my visual aids, I decided that this house would have a rusty tin roof, which is a variation of orange. Now I had the starting point for my color plan.

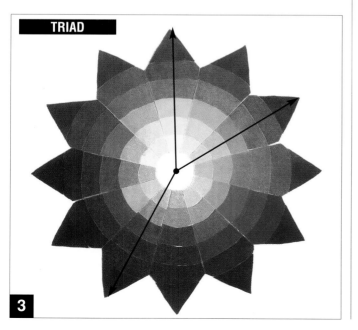

3 Pick your color harmony with the help of a color star. Once you've made decisions about the dominant colors in your rug, it's time to see if you have the start of a color harmony. I always have a color star handy when I'm at this stage of planning a rug. Can you see the harmony emerging in my rug? The colors selected to this point are yellow and orange. These are just a step apart on the color star, so I had the start of a split complement. In this harmony, the third color has to be blue-purple, which is perfect for the sky. Thousands of artists have proven that the split complement is appealing, so I had reduced the risk that the rug's color plan would go awry.

48

4 Continue making color decisions. To create variety, look for light and dark values of the hues that are in your harmony. The color star is a good reference for this. Place your finger on the point of one of the colors in your harmony. As you slide your finger toward the center of the star, you pass a wide range of colors that you can use to color plan your rug.

For my rug, I was challenged with finding colors for the fields and the hills that weren't too similar, but still stayed within the established harmony. Because I'm working with the split-complement of only yellow, orange and blue-purple, all of the fields and hills had to be either dark values of orange or yellow (the "green" used here is a dark value of yellow) or both orange and yellow. The flowers will be worked in leftover wools that aren't all the same value. The green and brown sunflower leaves come from a stew of yellow and orange. Small pieces of a dark value yellow plaid (green) are used in the sunflower centers.

5 I used a left over gray wool that was overdyed with orange for the tin roof. To create continuity throughout the work, this meant I had to include orange wools of varying values and intensities elsewhere, like in the chimney and rooster. For interest, the tin roof and sky wools were spot dyed. The house wool is from a brown stew (see page 27), created to resemble the colors found in weathered wood. The first element I hooked was the house. I didn't do the door because I wasn't sure what color I wanted it. I started with orange, but decided that I didn't want the door to stand out as much. By the time this rug was finished, I had reverse-hooked the door (pulled out loops) twice!

6 Choose colors for the remaining pattern elements. It's important to have variety while remaining true to your rug's color harmony. (But do remember that it's okay to choose colors that aren't in the harmony, because theory is a tool to be used with your ability to make good color decisions.)

Because my rug's harmony only uses yellow, orange, and blue-purple, the colors I picked for the fields, hills, and sky had to come from these choices. The sky is a light value of blue-purple, and I added an orange tint to the white wool used for the clouds.

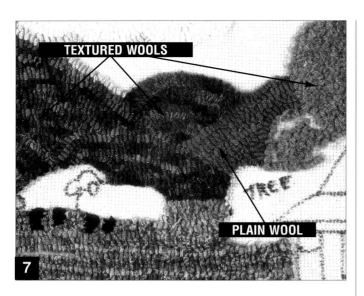

7 Carry your harmony through the wool colors. I managed to stick to the harmony for the rug shown in these steps by introducing yellow into each wool that I used for the hills.

The four hills all feature dark values of yellow (green). The two larger hills—one on the right side of the rug and one on the left—were hooked in a circular pattern using a blue-gray plaid wool that was overdyed with yellow to make it appear green. The hill behind the house and tree is a plain dark yellow wool that lacks texture. It anchors the hills. The smallest hill is an as-is plaid in a very dark value of yellow. Next I had to pick colors for the fields in the center of the rug. I used an as-is yellow plaid in the field where the sheep are grazing. As I moved down to the lower field, I introduced a very subtle orange and yellow plaid that blended with the other plaid.

8 Add new colors as needed. As you already know, yellow is the dominant color in my rug. The sunflowers are pure yellows, while the fields and hills are grayed yellows that I call the "green" of yellow. Even the sunflower centers, which contain a tiny bit of orange, contain two yellow values. So what do you think I used for the pea gravel house path? It's yellow, of course. In this case, the wool is a gray plaid that also contains light yellow.

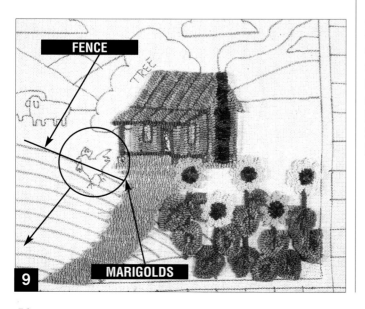

9 Personalize the pattern. Compare the original pattern for *Lamb's Tongues and Sunflowers* to the finished piece, both shown on page 47. I moved the rooster, plus added a pot of marigolds and a fence festooned with morning glories. (See step 12 for more discussion about these two elements.) I wanted a summer scene, so the smoke coming from the chimney had to go. (Who has a blazing fire in the hearth when flowers are in full bloom?) Then I decided that the rooster needed to move to the ploughed field at bottom left. I knew that he'd be happier there.

Not Easy Being Green

What do you do when hills and trees are next to one another? You need contrast but, if you're a traditionalist like me, you prefer to use colors that are found in nature. This is one of the challenges I faced with the *Lamb's Tongues and Sunflowers* pattern. I had to figure out a way to keep the tree from looking like a hill! I started with a cream and orange plaid, and then overdyed it with blue. Hooray! The final wool color gave me enough contrast to the sky and hills.

10 Do a trial run. When I'm teaching, I sometimes ask students to cut wool shapes and place them on a pattern, to fine-tune the color plan. This is a great way to help them get a better understanding of color harmony. This isn't a foolproof method, but it's a good way to discover that something isn't working before you spend time hooking an area. Simply pin your pattern to a foam core board, cut shapes from your wool choices, pin your shapes to the pattern, and then take a look. It's very important that you hang the pattern and step back to assess the effect. You can't visualize something when it's flat. Pay particular attention to value contrast. Without this, you can use all the right colors and still not have a successful plan.

11 Keep an open mind. At this point, most hookers would work the sheep since they're forward motifs. I didn't, because I was debating hooking them with something other than wool. Besides, if I decided to use wool, I didn't want the white sheep discolored by the other wools. I almost always debate a few parts of the design as I hook . . . and I always remain open to change. The rug was well underway, for example, when I finalized the rooster colors.

Quick-Start Questionnaire

As you pick the colors and hook the pattern for a rug, you can maintain an attractive piece by continually asking yourself the following questions:

- Are my colors good neighbors and good contrast to one another?
- Do I have enough contrast in color values and pattern details?
- Am I maintaining good balance with the color values and details?
- Am I using repetition of color to give continuity to my work?
- Is my expression of color imaginative?
- Have I used a little exaggeration to give oomph to some details?

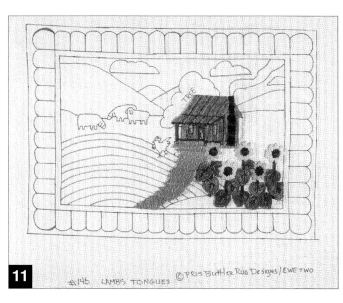

12 Establish triangles of color. The lowland houses in South Carolina always have flowers, so I personalized my rug a bit more. Now there's a rusty old tin full of marigolds in front of the house. This motif is worked in orange and yellow so that it fits into the color plan. Balancing colors and pattern elements is an ongoing process. For example, I added a fence above the ploughed field to give this portion of the rug contrast and movement. My love of flower gardening and desire for color balance led me to automatically hook morning glories on the fence. Now the rug has a triangular balance of blue. You can visualize the triangle by looking at the sky, the tree behind the house, and the flowers on the fence. I don't consider the blue in the lamb's tongues border to be part of the color balance.

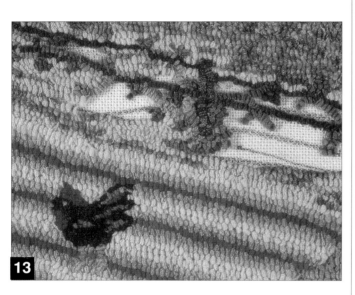

13 Add the third color of your color harmony. The field at bottom left bothered me. I already knew that hooking it with dark and light colors would make it look like a plowed field. It needed to be very different from all the other fields and hills. A total change of color and exaggerated lines of directional hooking achieved the desired effect. Yet I still stuck to the rug's color harmony by working the ridges with dark orange wool strips. A golden brown and a lighter orange-brown were used in the furrows. Although there's a touch of orange in the rooster, this bird really needed some red. I gave him just the spark that he needed without straying far from the color harmony. You can move out of a color harmony if you think a change will help a rug look better.

14 Add texture to dead space. The field to the right of the house isn't dramatic. After all, rugs do need a place for the eye to rest. A quiet spot isn't the same as dead space. You need to use textures, like plaids and tweeds, or several values of one color to prevent an area from looking too flat. I used two tweeds together simply to break up the space. There's also directional hooking that's hardly noticeable, yet it's enough to give the field some movement.

15

15 Abandon colors that aren't working. I wrestled the dragon when I was hooking the border. He almost won. For the lamb's tongues, you want to pull colors from the rug pattern that are pleasant to look at, but not the first thing you notice. Some people make great choices simply by laying out colors. I can't do that. I have to play . . . hook a bit and see what happens. One lamb's tongue is enough for me to make a decision. For this book, however, I hooked more so that you can see the effect. The dark orange and golden brown from the field, a green from the sunflower leaves, another green from the hills, and a blue from the tree worked out well. The fine line of bright yellow in the center stood out like a bulls eye! I tried a green from the field that the sheep are in, but finally settled for a spot-dyed wool in a lighter value of yellow. The curb line wasn't too difficult. I always use an uneven number of lines, because this arrangement is more visually pleasing. In this case, the blue from the tree and green from the sunflower leaves link the border to the rug pattern.

▶TIP My Hidden Identity

Make certain you identify your hooked pieces. Before you begin to hook, put your name on the back side of your pattern using a RUB-A-DUB pen (laundry marker). Determine a place that you would use for every hooked piece, like the lower left corner. You will cover it over when you hook, but you will know how to prove it is yours if your piece is ever lost or stolen.

Of course, add your initials and date (or dates, if it takes you years to finish a piece) on the front of the rug. The placement of dates and initials is personal. I like my identification to be subtle, so I might try to hide my initials in stems or tendrils, or discreetly among the leaves. Sometimes that isn't possible; then, I place them in a balanced position in the design.

Use identifying labels on the back of your pieces. They should contain this information:
- Name of the pattern
- Name of the designer
- Who hooked the piece: "Hooked by _____"
- Type of backing (burlap, linen, monk's cloth, rug warp)
- Materials used (as is new wool, as is recycled wool, custom dyed wool, and other materials)

Memory Marker

We all need help when we have so many colors and different wools to track as we're color planning. I have a little trick that's a very good way to remember where all of the colors will go in any rug that I hook. I simply cut a short strip of the assigned wool and pull it through the backing somewhere on the pattern element I want to be that color.

Bed Rug Fantasy, 50" x 40", #6-cut wool on monk's cloth. Designed by Marie Azzaro. Hooked by Betty Krull, Greer, South Carolina, 1994.

Rug hookers often ask me, "Where do I start?" Usually, they're staring at a pattern printed on a backing and are sometimes overwhelmed with too much wool and too many color choices. Earlier in this chapter, I walked you through the process I used for getting started on one rug. That section, called the "Process in Action" offers practical advice that's based on color theory. The information on the remaining pages in this chapter explains in further detail how you can use color theory to plan a rug.

This is the wallpaper that inspired *Bed Rug Fantasy*. My first color choice was a rich, deep blue for the background. To this, we added several values of reds and incorporated some red to khaki dip-dyes. The light color of khaki-tan was dyed with a mix of khaki and maroon. The use of this last color adds a unique element of interest. The surprise is the greens, which were dyed with a bright green bleeder. (A bleeder is a piece of wool that isn't suitable for hooking, but is very valuable as a dye source. Placed in a pot with other wools, the color in the bleeder will seep into the other fabrics. See Stew Dyeing on page 27.)

Museum Bed Rug, 50" x 40", #6-cut wool on monk's cloth. Designed by Marie Azzaro. Hooked by Betty Krull, Greer, South Carolina, 1990.

Color theory is a tool. It'll make it easier to plan a rug, but I don't want anyone to think that it's the only way to get started. *Bed Rug Fantasy*, shown on page 54, was planned to match some wallpaper that my youngest daughter liked.

This rug, which was designed by Marie Azzaro, is a copy of a style of old motifs that continues to fascinate me.

We aimed for a balanced relationship of all the elements, from color and fabric to the pattern itself. Then we included unique elements of interest and even surprise.

Whatever your color favorites or cultural influences, certain theories about planning a rug hold true. All relate to the essential elements of good design, which are interest, proportion, rhythm and unity.

Interest

Put in its simplest terms, interest is little more than the variety of chromas, colors, and values that you use in a rug. Your rug doesn't have to have a wide range of colors to be successful. Contrasting values and chromas (the purity or intensity of a color), preferably in unequal intervals and amounts, will do the trick.

When a rug doesn't have enough difference in its intensities and values, it lacks appeal. Interesting color combinations use fewer colors, but a wider variety of intensities and values.

▶ **TIP Interesting Ideas**

When you want to add interest through fabric choice, consider some of the following options:
- Many checks and plaids are available today. You can use them as-is, or else overdye them as desired.

- Salt shaker dyeing
- Casserole, dip, and spot dyeing all add variety to wool strips.
- Vary the chroma by using a classic six- or eight-value swatch.

Consider the portion of the *Museum Bed Rug* shown on page 55. Each of the red flowers has eight or nine values that range from dark to medium to bright. While all five look similar, unequal intervals of values and intensities of one color provide enough variety to keep them from looking like five red-fried eggs. This treatment is the only way that you can make a large flower interesting.

Placing two high intensity colors together won't introduce interest because the colors are too similar. Even a very light value beside a high intensity is not pleasing because the high intensity element can draw attention completely away from the light value.

Interest can be introduced through your fabric choices. Of course, the type of hooking you do may limit your flexibility in this area, because your style determines the amount of texture that you can use. Traditional tapestry hooking, using a fine-cut of wool, requires smooth fabric with a tight weave. On the other hand, you can have a grand time with primitive or folk art pieces because a wide-cut lends itself easily to plaids and other interesting textures like herringbone woolens and tweeds. (Make sure that your backing will accommodate the wool cut that you've decided to use.)

Interest can also be accomplished with exaggeration. In fact, this is sometimes necessary to give a color plan more character. Exaggeration can be in a dominant detail or a grouping of smaller details. You achieve the effect with directional lines of hooking in an element of the design, or by using a high intensity color in an area.

Proportion

Color areas should be unequal. The rug shown above, for example, is based on a red, yellow, and blue triad. Note how red hues are used the most in this piece. Even the background is a very dark value of red. There's a bit less yellow, and blue is used the least.

For more information about this piece, *Antique Rose*, see page 64.

I'd like to say that experts all agree on the ideal proportions for colors in a work, but it isn't possible. Thomas Gainsborough, who painted the famous Blue Boy portrait, believed the ideal color balance is 2/3 cool and 1/3 warm. In direct contradiction, Sir Joshua Reynolds, another portrait painter and Gainsborough's contemporary, said the ideal proportion is 2/3 warm and 1/3 cool. What's a rug hooker to do?

My rule of thumb is that a large area of color needs to be balanced by three or four smaller spots worked in the same color but different values, chromas, or both. (Proportion can relate to amounts of color, and even the balance of cool and warm.) If the largest area is a higher chroma, balance it with smaller areas of lower chromas, which may be in several different values. The three or four smaller areas should equal the size of the largest area. Keep in mind that the eye is disturbed by a lack of balance.

"The success of any color combination depends on the use of colors that are well enough related to make an attractive whole but different enough to provide the variety needed to dispel any sense of monotony."—
Author Unknown

Oyster Bay Antique, 63" x 37", #6-cut wool on monk's cloth. Designed by Louise Hunter Zeiser. Hooked by Betty Krull, Greer, South Carolina, 1993.

"Harmonious color plans rely on an individually pleasing relationship of the three classifications of color— hue, value, and intensity. Personal taste and preference must also be considered.—Author Unknown

Rhythm and Unity

Rhythm and unity are closely related and both are achieved with repetition, be it through color, line, shape, or any combination of these elements.

Oyster Bay Antique, the rug show above, is an excellent example of rhythm and unity. The comma shape of the cornucopia is repeated in the background and the border motifs.

In rug hooking, rhythm and unity depend on color paths (see page 21). One of the most valuable tools for achieving unity and rhythm is the theory of triangular balance. This is a fairly easy concept to understand, and it's one that artists have used for centuries to bring movement and unity to their work. When color planning your rug, simply ensure that a single color is placed at points throughout the work where, if you joined the points with a line, you'd have a triangle. You don't need a lot of color at each location.

I chose the above pattern when my oldest daughter asked for a purple rug. The two cornucopias caught my attention. The challenge was to make them look old and weathered, like antique basketry. I lost track of the amount of wool I dyed that didn't work.

The border design of repeating comma shapes was developed in a class taught by Jule Marie Smith at Green Mountain Rug School in Montpelier, Vermont. I used a casserole dye over very long strips of wool with red, yellow, blue and purple dye blended into each other. The background is hooked in comma shapes for subtle movement.

▶**TIP Special Memories**

The welcome rug at my front door is a memory rug—not because of the design but because of the wool I used. All the wool in that rug has a story—A daughter's skirt from her first year in college; my WOW black wool suit; red from one of my favorite red winter coats; left-over wool from the first sport coat I made for my husband; wool from the girls' coats that I made for them when they were small; and leftover wool from many of my braided rugs. It's fun to hook and to have special pieces like this.

CHAPTER FIVE

Visiting the Gallery

There's nothing like looking at a wide variety of rugs to get the creative juices flowing. Well, there's one thing that's better . . . talking with the designers and learning more about the color decisions and challenges that they faced when they hooked each particular piece.

In this gallery of finished rugs, you're getting the ultimate tour. You'll find photos and commentary on almost two-dozen pieces. Some rugs are my work, others belong to my friends and students.

It's my hope that showing you these rugs will help familiarize you with the color harmonies and the many ways that they can be interpreted.

Many of my rugs were hooked for myself, or my children, before I developed The Color Course. The color plans for some of them aren't based on a harmony. It's important that you know this. I don't want anyone to think that a rug isn't good if it doesn't start with a color harmony. The message I hope that you get from The Secrets of Color in Hand-Hooked Rugs is that color theory will make it easier to select rug colors.

The gallery of finished rugs also includes a handful of pieces that were worked from one pattern, called Coventry. The color plans for every one of them were developed at a rug hooking school in 2003, where several students were interested in learning more about color.

Museum Bed Rug, 50" x 40", #6-cut wool on monk's cloth. Designed by Marie Azzaro. Hooked by Betty Krull, Greer, South Carolina, 1990.

This is one of my favorite rugs. It's a triad that uses blue, yellow, and red. At the time I made it, wide-cut rugs weren't that acceptable. I was fortunate that I made it while at Green Mountain Rug School, Montpelier, Vermont. The rug school is held at Vermont Technical College in Randolph Center.

Jean Armstrong was my teacher and I'm so glad that she was there for my first attempt at a wide-cut rug. She suggested the lamb's ear border, which is a nice finishing touch.

All of the reds are from a stew, and were stacked in the pot in the following order, from bottom to top: wine, red, gray flannel, dark bright red, gray tweed, rusty red, another gray flannel, and pink and white. I always put a piece of white wool on top of every stew that I make. This is wonderful way to build a collection of off-white wool. The blues are blue, blue check, and gray tweed overdyed with navy. The gold background will never be repeated. I played with old ivory, old gold, taupe, golden brown, a gold formula in an unmarked jar, and some red. So much for keeping dye records.

I chose this pattern when my oldest daughter asked for a purple rug. The two cornucopias caught my attention. The challenge was to make them look old and weathered, like antique basketry. I lost track of the amount of wool I dyed that didn't work.

The border design, repeating comma shapes, was developed in a class taught by Jule Marie Smith at Green Mountain Rug School in Montpelier, Vermont. I used a casserole dye over very long strips of wool with red, yellow, blue, and purple dye blended into each other. The background is hooked in comma shapes for subtle movement.

Oyster Bay Antique, 37" x 63", #6-cut wool on monk's cloth. Designed by Louise Hunter Zeiser. Hooked by Betty Krull, Greer, South Carolina, 1993.

Winchester Chair Pad companion piece, 14" in diameter, #6-cut wool on burlap. Designed by Jane McGown Flynn. Hooked by Betty Krull, Greer, South Carolina, 1998.

I've been a flower gardener much longer than I've been a rug hooker. When I began to garden in the South, I quickly learned the value of white flowers. They give my garden a sense of coolness. My dream is a white flower garden with an herb border. Since this has never come about, *Winchester* became that garden.

The challenge always with white flowers is to keep them white. Because we need contrast and shadows, it's very easy to use color with too much intensity. When this happens, you end up with colored—not white—flowers. The border is hooked in the gray-green that you see in most herbs, with hints of color at the tips. The black-brown background enhances the drama of the white flowers.

This rug was my first teaching assignment at the Southern Teacher's Workshop, in Ripley, West Virginia. The chair pad is the companion piece, and uses motifs taken from the rug. This small version was taught in a one-day class at the workshop.

Winchester, 44" x 88", #6-cut wool on monk's cloth. Designed by Jane McGown Flynn. Hooked by Betty Krull, Greer, South Carolina, 1998.

It's always a pleasure to plan and hook a rug that's just for me. I love to be free to choose the colors and patterns that'll look best in my home. But the reality is that, as a teacher, I also need to hook pieces that show my students something that I'm explaining in one of my classes. There are times when I can use one of the rugs that I hooked as a teaching tool, but this isn't always possible.

Turkish Kilim was hooked specifically as a teaching tool for my class. This class was the starting point for *The Secrets of Color in Hand-Hooked Rugs*. I show the pillow to students as an example of the use of traditional colors in a hooked piece.

I love the color plan. The reds are dynamic, the golds have an earthy quality, and the browns are earth tones. It was a fun and easy piece to hook.

Turkish Kilim, 14" x 14", #3-cut wool on burlap. Designed by Jane McGown Flynn. Hooked by Betty Krull, Greer, South Carolina, 2000.

Kneeling Bench, 19" x 8", #3-cut wool on rug warp. Designer unknown. Hooked by Betty Krull, Greer, South Carolina, 1998.

I have a passion for stools . . . ask anyone who antiques with me. This long bench is a style known as a kneeling bench. It's from an old church in Arlington, Massachusetts. The crewel design was copied from a free pattern that I found in a very old *Early American Life* magazine. I adapted it to fit this stool and just had fun.

This darling piece is a one-dollar flea market find that I painted white. The pattern was a joy to make. All it took was some backing, cookie cutters, and scrap wool. Not necessarily a work of art and it was fun and hooked in my most favorite place, my porch. Rug hooking should be fun!

The colors in this piece—red, white, and blue—aren't classified by a particular harmony. Nevertheless, they are harmonious because they're pleasing to the eye.

My Stars, 8 ¹/₂" x 6", #5-cut wool on burlap. Designed and hooked by Betty Krull, Greer, South Carolina, 1998.

The design for this rug is simple: a basket of flowers and a wreath of flowers. Hooking the basket in wools from a brown stew gives the simple design status as an antique. Simple flowers are worked from an assortment of as-is wools that Louise brought to the class that I taught. They're hooked against a navy background. It was created with solid navy and navy plaid wools that were cooked and then hooked together. No dye was added.

We had such fun seeing how many small pieces of wool we could use, like the little bit of plaid that was just enough for the centers of the two yellow flowers in the wreath. Playing greens against other greens added to our most pleasant experience.

Louise and I both love the combination of colors that we achieved. The finished rug is a beautiful piece of folk art.

Flower Basket, 44" x 28", #7-cut wool on rug warp. Design comes from a book written by Leslie Linsley, *Hooked Rugs: An American Folk Art,* published by Clarkson N. Potter. Hooked by Louise Schram, Whitehouse, Ohio, 2002.

Betty's Petticoat, 11 ¹/₂" x 47 ¹/₂", #3-cut wool on monk's cloth. Designed and hooked by Joyce Krueger, Waukesha, Wisconsin, 2003.

This design was taken from the crewel work on an antique petticoat. Three Betty's were involved in the process of design, color planning, and hooking. I helped choose the split complementary color harmony of blue green, orange, and red. Betty McClentic was the teacher at the Chicago Teacher's Workshop who got everything off to a good start with the beautiful light and dark values of the central feather motif. What a lovely illusion of movement these values create. Time spent with Betty Laine provided information on the need for a main color, a secondary color, and an accent color.

For traditional crewel, it's necessary to use all three colors and move them into each motif. The end result is spectacular. How sad it would be to hide this petticoat!

Chat Noir, 24" x 36", #3-cut wool on monk's cloth. Designed by Jane McGown Flynn. Hooked by Terrill Persky, Naperville, Illinois, 2003.

When Terrill began planning this rug, she talked about using yellow-green for the leaves. Her other color choices were purple and blue, so the leaf color would, perhaps, have been acceptable. I'm glad that she revised her color plan. The sophisticated effect of a bronze, a yellow-orange, is much better. It also better suits the Art Nouveau design. (Art Nouveau designs and motifs are in a class all their own.)

After you've picked colors for a rug, don't shut the door on revisions. You may change your mind when you see how each wool looks when worked into a rug. Even the color plan for the rug featured in the Color Planning chapter, which I made specifically to show you the process, went through a few changes before completion.

PRO Chem dye #503 came through this time . . . yielding a lovely pale lavender for the background. (Color #503 is elusive, we're just never sure what we'll end up with.) Terrill says the end result is subtle and elegant, just what she had hoped for.

Pumpkin Boy, 35" x 24", #6-cut wool on linen. Designed by Melody Hoops. Hooked by Betty Krull, Greer, South Carolina, 2000.

This rug proves my point that theory is the tool, but we still need to trust our own judgment and imagination. *Pumpkin Boy* began as a study of analogous colors. I chose yellow-green, yellow, yellow-orange, orange, orange-red, and red. I loved everything about the color plan. The dark pumpkin was hooked with the wool from an orange plaid shirt; the middle pumpkin was hooked with a spot dye and the light pumpkin used up lots of odds and ends of orange wool. The *Pumpkin Boy* sweater was hooked from a small piece of plaid wool and his overalls were worked in brown. At this point, my whole concept of analogous colors went out the window. It's quite all right to move away from a color harmony. Using your own colors and your discerning eye is always acceptable in rug hooking.

The overalls had to be blue with orange stitching—and the bird—had to be blue. The bird on the scarecrow's hat is a very rare pumpkin breasted blue bird . . . the only one of its kind.

I started *Antique Rose* when I needed another visual aid for my class, The Color Course. The pattern is from a book that I inherited from my aunt, who was also a rug hooker. I wanted to create a triadic color harmony (see page 42).

I decided on the red, yellow, blue triad. Every color decision that I made was based on a favorite background wool. It's a red plaid wool shirt that I overdyed with black and maroon.

The rest of the wool was as-is pieces that came from my aunt's collection.

I knew the center rose had to be red. I used yellow variations for the leaves, the green or dark values of yellow, because green isn't in the triad.

The yellow became the secondary color with small touches of blue in small flowers. The corner motifs repeat the yellow—and blue colors. The red of the plaid shirt sparkles in the background. My love of red is certainly obvious in this rug.

Antique Rose, 38" x 24", #6-cut wool on rug warp. Pattern from *Hooked Rugs: A Historical and Collector's Guide: How to Make Your Own* by William C. Ketchum Jr, published by Harcourt Brace Jovanovich. Hooked by Betty Krull, Greer, South Carolina, 2003.

Country Village is the kind of pictorial that invites you to be creative. Using this pattern, I took a class with Kerri Forfinski at the Southern Teacher's Workshop in Ripley, West Virginia. She depicted an autumn scene. At the same workshop, I also took a class with Irene Kemner, called Snowed In. When I was back home, I translated *Country Village* into a wintry New England scene by hooking lots of snow. I also added children having fun out-doors.

I used a complementary color harmony of blue and orange. The orange was dyed over gray wool for a nice, warm brown. The clouds are a spot dye that uses very light values of blue and orange.

Country Village, 36" x 24", #6-cut wool on monk's cloth. Designed by Jane McGown Flynn. Hooked by Betty Krull, Greer, South Carolina, 2000.

I used lots of as-is wool for clothes, houses, and trees. The mountains were hooked with a gray-and-white block plaid. This is a rug, not a wall hanging, so I flattened the metal bell in the church steeple.

This is an analogous color harmony covering the color circle from yellow-green through purple. With this wide range of colors, the key is to keep the eye moving and the colors anchored together. You don't want a piece to be disjointed, with jumps from color to color. You do want to see individual colors, but the overall effect should be one of beauty and movement.

The range of colors from green through to blue is great for imparting the illusion of motion. My friend, Joyce, allowed the remaining colors to enhance the overall beauty of the rug.

The use of transcolor swatches (see page 24) and closely related values creates the flowing look and feel of the rug; while the deep blue background anchors the design with its wide variety of colors and many intensities and values. In a recent magazine article I saw a room planned with all the light value (tints) of this rug. It was lovely, and I thought about how this rug would look as an accent piece in that color plan. The whole image was so restful—the characteristics of the color range achieve that feeling. Add a comfortable rocking chair—delightful!

Coventry, 36" x 24", #6-cut wool on rug warp. Designed by Katherine Porter. Hooked by Joyce Krueger, Waukesha, Wisconsin, 2003.

Neville Sisters Crewel, 28" x 49", #3-cut wool on burlap. Designed by Jane McGown Flynn. Hooked by Betty Krull, Greer, South Carolina, 1989.

Beshir, 12" x 20", #3-cut on burlap. Designed by Jane McGown Flynn. Hooked by Betty Krull, Greer, South Carolina, 1999.

Traditional designs like this crewel pattern have always been my favorite. This is still one of the hooked pieces that I like the most for both the colors and the design. But there's another reason why it'll always hold a special place in my heart: it was the second rug that I ever hooked. Sentimental favorites will always win out with me.

When I started *Neville Sisters Crewel* I never realized that parts of the hooking would be so challenging. To maintain the shape and size of the repeats for the Greek key and ribbon motifs I had to count the rows of hooking as I worked.

I've always been one to jump right into a project, learning to swim as the work progressed. I guess this is part of my creative personality.

When I was asked to teach The Color Course the first time at the Southern Teacher's Workshop in Ripley, West Virginia, the assigned pattern was *Beshir*.

Given its content, it would be natural to use oriental colors for *Beshir*. Instead, I decided to stretch myself by working it a bit differently. This pattern became a teaching tool for The Color Course that I teach. Arranged around a central axis are four repeated designs. I worked each repeat in a different color harmony: analogous, complementary, monochromatic, and triadic.

As you can imagine, the wool colors were critical; I spent hours with my dye pots and wools. The colors needed to flow into each other. This isn't a project I would like to repeat but, like so many things in life, I'm glad I did it once.

On the warm side of the color wheel is a span of analogous colors. I used the yellow-orange, orange, red-orange, and red range to make a dramatic statement. The intensity of the colors gives this analogous harmony its impact.

People say that the flowers in my rug glow. I love it when they notice this. This wonderful effect, called iridescence, is achieved through the strategic placement of colors, so that one plays off

Coventry, 36" x 24", #6-cut wool on rug warp. Designed by Katherine Porter. Hooked by Betty Krull, Greer, South Carolina, 2003.

another. In this case, I did it by combining red with closely related values of orange.

Dark values and shades of yellow-orange with gray provide a look we want to identify as green in the large leaves. The central leaves are orange, in the deep tones that most people know as brown. This striking color harmony is anchored against another brown (a dark red) background. Some colors need to be grounded so that they don't appear to float off the rug.

When Susanne said she wanted to try something different, she wasn't kidding. Beginning with orange, she crossed over the center of the color star to the complement, and then chose the colors on either side. The result is a split complement with blue-purple and blue-green.

Her rug is a beautiful example of a great way to use more values and intensities, not more colors. The orange has 10 variations, including an tint for the background, plus some overdyed plaids and oatmeal wools. There are 12 variations of the blue-green,

Coventry, 36" x 24", #6-cut wool on rug warp. Designed by Katherine Porter. Hooked by Susanne McNally, Gibsonia, Pennsylvania, 2003.

which also includes overdyed plaids and checks. The smallest amount of color is the blue-purple, used in a variety in colors and amounts. All three colors (orange, blue-purple, and blue-green) were used in a spot dye. Because the background is light, Susanne bordered her rug with several rows of the dark orange, what many would call brown, to anchor the rug.

When we think of red and green, Christmas immediately comes to mind. This is the danger of some color schemes. Think of Easter and pastels immediately come to mind. Or, as you can see in the *My Stars* pattern for the stool on page 62 a patriotic theme immediately comes to mind when you pull together red, white, and blue.

But Louise was able to eliminate that seasonal aura even though she hooked a dramatic red and green complementary color harmony.

The leaves are hooked with texture and grayed values. A stew made from an assortment of green wools—both solids and plaids—and black wool were used for the background. Both the leaves and background are equally important for anchoring the reds. A curb line hooked with a red spot dye is just enough of a break between the dark green center and the outer black border. The red flowers glow like stars against the many intensities and values green.

Coventry, 36" x 24", #6-cut wool on linen. Designed by Katherine Porter. Hooked by Louise Schram, Whitehouse, Ohio, 2003.

I fell in love with New England when I moved there as a bride, and it didn't take long to develop an enthusiasm for antiques—an enthusiasm that continues today. This rug is a copy of a style of old motifs that continue to fascinate me.

Bed Rug Fantasy was color planned to match the wallpaper in my youngest daughter's home. I love the intensity of the greens, which are true to colors of the period of the bed ruggs. The greens in this piece were dyed with a bleeder.

A bleeder is a piece of wool that isn't suitable for hooking, but is very valuable as a dye source. Placed in a pot with other wools, the color in the bleeder will seep into the other fabrics.

A blue stew also included a piece of an orange-and-cream plaid blanket. (This is the same wool that I used for the tree behind the house in the *Lamb's Tongues and Sunflowers* rug shown on page 47.) The blanket wool became a green that worked well with the color harmony of this rug.

Bed Rug Fantasy, 50" x 40", #6-cut wool on monk's cloth. Designed by Marie Azzaro. Hooked by Betty Krull, Greer, South Carolina, 1994.

A double complementary harmony needs a wide range of color. For Marilyn's interpretation of the *Coventry* pattern, this means using colors in the red-green and blue-orange spectrums.

However, this rug was color planned using only two swatches. One of the swatches, which goes from blue to orange, was the first choice. This is called a transcolor, or transitional, swatch because it changes from one color to another. Where the blue starts shifting to orange, we obtained a variation of blue that's gray-green. We then extended this eight-value swatch to twelve values by adding clear color at both ends. A red swatch added to the orange/blue swatch completed the color harmony.

Marilyn and I included some overdyed tweeds. A navy blue wool, overdyed with bright green and chartreuse, was the perfect backdrop for the rich and subtle colors used in this harmony.

Coventry, 36" x 24", #6-cut wool on rug warp. Designed by Katherine Porter. Hooked by Marilyn Denning, Burlington, Wisconsin, 2003.

This was a required hooked piece for my accreditation as a certified McGown teacher. At the workshop, this was called my "show and tell." I used this piece to test my ability to develop my own dye formulas. The work shows a method of moving color from one motif to another, a technique used in traditional crewel work. In this case, colors that are commonly used in crewel—blue, gold, red, and yellow-greens—are worked into my *Pett Bell Pull*. The year that I created this piece, I wasn't able to attend the workshop. Instead, I wrote a poem about the work and sent that along. (See page 70.)

Rug hooking has been an important part of my life for a very long time. It has been a challenging and satisfying activity. Nothing else has come close to fulfilling my desire for creative expression. And I love being able to help hookers create rugs that others want to look at again and again. But, above all else, rug hooking has—and continues to be—fun. In my classes, I often remind students of that. So don't let yourself get too caught up in a struggle for the perfect color plan, and trust your instincts.

Pett Bell Pull, 6" x 42", #3-cut wool on burlap. Designed by Jane McGown Flynn. Hooked by Betty Krull, Greer, South Carolina, 1993.

Pett Bell Pull

By Betty Krull

Walk with me in a whimsical garden
Where grows a most fanciful vine.
With berries and leaves, flowers and fruit
It resembles no garden of mine.

From dye pots just four the colors have come,
PRO Chem yellow, black, red, and blue.
Measured and tested while my cauldrons bubbled
As I searched for each perfect hue.

For the dominant focus, only red will do
As along the vine it dances.
No ingénue, red; it calls for applause
And always, your most pleasing glances.

Shadings of blue are like rare China silk
Intense, never fading from sight.
Accents of gold, the color of riches
Azure leaves enhance our delight.

Purple is regal, perhaps even aloof,
'Til lighthearted bells gently sway.
Among leaves of green, both bright and brassy,
As upward this vine grows each day.

My whimsical vine here now is displayed
By hook and wool colors sublime.
Jack has his beanstalk, a legend of yore;
But no matter . . . now, I have mine.

Sources

The following is a list of sources for the many materials and techniques discussed in this book. Keep in mind that this is only a partial list of the many companies that sell these products. Most of these companies, and many more, advertise in Rug Hooking *magazine. These companies can get you started with all the supplies you need to make hand-hooked rugs. The rest is up to you. Enjoy!*

Rug Hooking Magazine
1300 Market Street, Suite 202
Lemoyne, PA 17043-1420
(800) 233-9055
rughook@paonline.com
www.rughookingonline.com
The indispensable source of rug hooking, dye, technique, and other information and advertisers. Annual subscription for just $27.95.

Castle in the Clouds
7108 Panavista Lane
Chattanooga, TN 37421
(423) 892-1858
castlerug@comcast.net
www.geocities.com/castlerug
Fleecewood Farm Patterns, including *Pumpkin Boy.*

Cross Creek Farm Rug School
Burton, Ohio
Beth Croup
13440 Taylor Wells Road
Chardon, OH 44024
(440) 635-0209
Workshops and Katherine Porter patterns, including *Coventry.*

Dorr Mill Store
PO Box 88
Guild, NH 03754
(800) 846-3677
dorrmillstore@sugar-river.net
www.dorrmillstore.com
Quality wools, color palettes, patterns, kits, and much more.

Green Mountain Hooked Rugs
Stephanie Ashworth Krauss
146 Main Street
Montpelier, VT 05602
(802) 223-1333
www.GreenMountainHookedRugs.com
Patterns, supplies, and the annual Green Mountain Rug School.

Harry M. Fraser Company
433 Duggins Road
Stoneville, NC 27048
(336) 573-9830
fraserrugs@aol.com
www.fraserrugs.com
Cloth-slitting machines, hooking, and braiding supplies.

Heirloom Rugs
124 Tallwood Drive
Vernon, CT 06066
(860) 870-8905
www.heirloomRUGS.com
Heirloom Designs patterns by Louise Hunter Zeiser and Margaret MacKenzie, including *Oyster Bay Antique.*

House of Price, Inc.
177 Brickyard Road
Mars, PA 16046-3001
(877) RUG-HOOK
rughook@earthlink.net
Fine quality hooking patterns, including Jane McGown Flynn's Charco designs for the following patterns: *Beshir, Bethlehem, Betty's Petticoat, Chat Noir, Country Village, Neville Sisters Crewel, Pett Bell Pull, Quaint, Summer Romance, Southwest III, Turkish Kilim,* and *Winchester.* Sponsor of the McGown Teacher Workshops, for those who wish to become accredited or want to refresh their skills.

Pris Buttler Rug Designs
PO Box 591
Oakwood ,GA 30566-0010
(770) 718-0090
prisrugs@charter.net
Pris Buttler patterns, including *Lamb's Tongues and Sunflowers.*

PRO Chemical & Dye
PO Box 14
Somerset, MA 02726
(800) 228-9393
www.prochemical.com
Dyeing supplies.

Wood N Wool
6400 Canon Wren
Austin, TX 78746
(512) 431-0431
woodnwoolhooking@aol.com
www.woodnwoolrughooking.com
Makers of quality rug hooking supplies: frames, stands, and hooks.

Yankee Peddler
Marie Azzaro
267 Route 81
Killingworth, CT 06419
(860) 663-0526
Cutters, hand-dyed wool, hooks, and patterns, including *Museum Bed Rug* and *Bed Rug Fantasy.*

WHAT IS RUG HOOKING?

Some strips of wool. A simple tool. A bit of burlap. How ingenious were the women and men of ages past to see how such humble household items could make such beautiful rugs?

Although some form of traditional rug hooking has existed for centuries, this fiber craft became a fiber art only in the last 150 years. The fundamental steps have remained the same: A pattern is drawn onto a foundation, such as burlap or linen. A zigzag line of stitches is sewn along the foundation's edges to keep them from fraying as the rug is worked. The foundation is then stretched onto a frame, and fabric strips or yarn, which may have been dyed by hand, are pulled through it with an implement that resembles a crochet hook inserted into a wooden handle. The compacted loops of wool remain in place without knots or stitching. The completed rug may have its edges whipstitched with cording and yarn as a finishing touch to add durability.

Despite the simplicity of the basic method, highly intricate designs can be created with it. Using a multitude of dyeing techniques to produce unusual effects, or various hooking methods to create realistic shading, or different widths of wool to achieve a primitive or formal style, today's rug hookers have gone beyond making strictly utilitarian floor coverings to also make wallhangings, vests, lampshades, purses, pictorials, portraits, and more. Some have incorporated other kinds of needlework into their hooked rugs to fashion unique and fascinating fiber art that's been shown in museums, exhibits, and galleries throughout the world.

For a good look at what contemporary rug hookers are doing with yesteryear's craft—or to learn how to hook your own rug—pick up a copy of *Rug Hooking* magazine, or visit our web site at *www.rughookingonline.com*. Within the world of rug hooking—and *Rug Hooking* magazine—you'll find there's a style to suit every taste and a growing community of giving, gracious fiber artists who will welcome you to their gatherings.—*Ginny Stimmel*

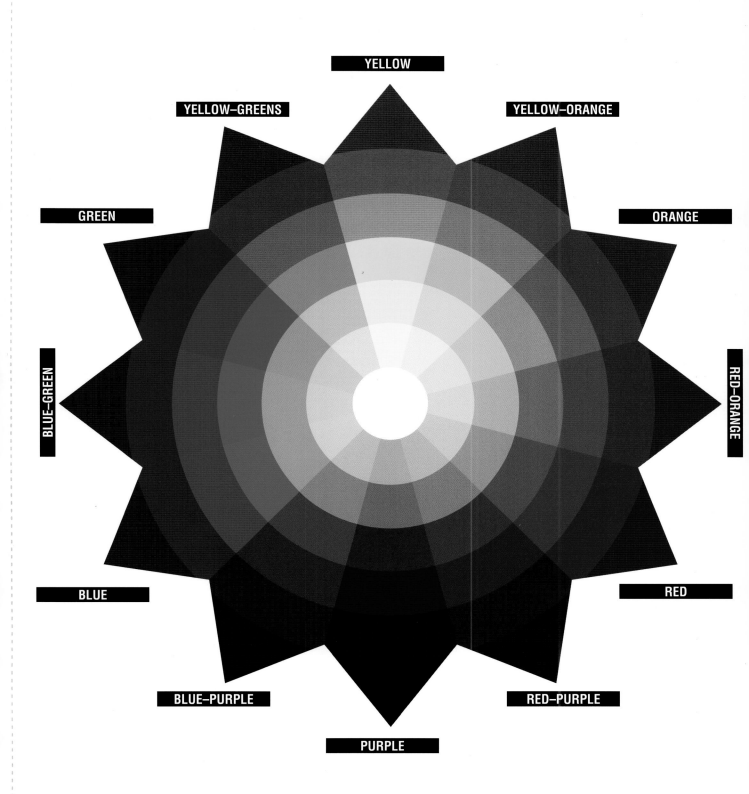

Primary Colors: Red, yellow, and blue.

Secondary Colors: Orange, green and purple.

Tertiary Colors or Intermediate Colors: A mix of primary and secondary colors, known as red-orange, yellow-orange, yellow-green, blue-green, blue-violet, and red-violet.

Monochromatic Harmony: This harmony is any one hue, used in a number of shades, tints, and tones. For a color plan based on one color, start with any hue on the color wheel. Concentrate on contrast: light, medium, and dark values of the hue. (See *The Secrets of Color in Hand-Hooked Rugs,* page 29).

Complementary Harmony: This harmony is any two colors that are directly opposite one another on the color star. Pick any color on a star or wheel, draw a line through it and across to the other side, and you have its opposite or complementary color. (See *The Secrets of Color in Hand-Hooked Rugs,* page 32).

Split Complementary Harmony: This color harmony uses one key color combined with two others that lay next to its exact opposite on the color star or wheel. It consists of three colors: any hue desired, plus the two that are beside its complement. (See *The Secrets of Color in Hand-Hooked Rugs,* page 34).

Double Complementary Harmony: This is a harmony of four, because the double complement uses two pairs of complements. There's one key color, its exact opposite, plus one other set of complements from any place on the color star. (See *The Secrets of Color in Hand-Hooked Rugs,* page 36).

Tetradic Harmony: This harmony is based on four hues evenly spaced around the color star. Choose a mix of primary, secondary, and tertiary hues. Use a rectangle or a square to determine the four colors. There's always one color between corners on each short side of the rectangle and three colors between the corners on the long sides of the rectangle. If you use a square, there will be two colors between the corner colors on each side. Where the corners end are the colors you'll use. (See T*he Secrets of Color in Hand-Hooked Rugs,* page 38).

Analogous Harmony: Analogous harmony can be seen in a rainbow. This scheme consists of several colors that are side-by-side on the color star or wheel. (See *The Secrets of Color in Hand-Hooked Rugs,* page 40).

Triadic Harmony: Any three colors that are equidistant on the color star make up a triadic harmony. (See *The Secrets of Color in Hand-Hooked Rugs,* page 42).